Sewing
With Knit Fabrics

Sewing
With Knit Fabrics

NANCY E. HOLLAND

SOUTH BRUNSWICK AND NEW YORK: A. S. BARNES AND COMPANY
LONDON: THOMAS YOSELOFF LTD

A. S. Barnes and Co., Inc.
Cranbury, New Jersey 08512

Thomas Yoseloff Ltd
108 New Bond Street
London W1Y OQX, England

Library of Congress Cataloging in Publication Data

Holland, Nancy E   1934—
   Sewing with knit fabrics.

   Includes index.
   1. Clothing and dress.   2. Sewing.   3. Knit goods.   I. Title.
TT557.H64   646.4'0028   74-30728
ISBN 0-498-01676-5

Illustrations by Ken Clayton

PRINTED IN THE UNITED STATES OF AMERICA

This book is dedicated to my family,
friends, and students
who inspired and encouraged me to write it.

Contents

Preface

Dear Home Fashion Creator,

Knits are delightful to wear and fun to sew. I am happy to share with you the techniques and skills that I use and have enjoyed sharing with my family, friends, and students. I had been hearing repeatedly from them, "Why don't you write a book and tell it (sewing knits) as you tell us." "It's so easy when you explain it." And so, I wrote this book that others might share in my mode of teaching and experience the exhilaration of self-accomplishment.

It is designed to kindle and enrich your knowledge of knits, and step by step, to accompany you from fabric selection to a completed wardrobe of timeless elegance. Part I will familiarize you with knit terminology and sewing preliminaries. Part II is an alphabetized presentation of knit sewing techniques. Part III contains practical applications of knit sewing techniques from underwear to beachwear.

Together we'll fashion a collection that fits the mood, the feeling, and the tempo of today. It might be wholly contemporary, beautifully classic, or a rich blend of both. It will be, unmistakably, a true work of art structured to last, and as truly distinctive as you, the Home Fashion Creator.

Acknowledgments

Many friends, colleagues, and chance acquaintances have extended kindness to me in the completion of this pursuit. For this I am grateful and would like to express my sincere appreciation to them and especially to:

Judi Blevins
Matthew B. McCormick
Pat Hearne
Madelon T. Aylwin
Sam Perdue
Nan Spence
Carol Whitney

Sewing
With Knit Fabrics

Part I

1

Know Your Knits

Unlike woven fabric, knits have the unique characteristics of stretchability, recoverability, wrinkle resistance, and ease of care. They stretch when your body demands more room and return to original size and shape when the crisis is over. Knits are subject to numerous fiber, structural, and finishing variances which affect the stretch, appearance, and texture of the fabric. They are, however, fundamentally formed by the same principle—successive, interlocking loops of yarn from one or more points of origin. Therein lies the key to why they are delightfully different and the biggest hit in the fashion world.

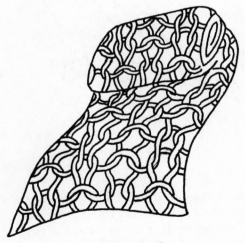

Interlocking yarn loops.

Knit fabrics fall into two classifications—weft knits and warp knits. Weft knits are produced by a knitting process and can be either flat or tubular. The yarn or yarns run in the weft direction, which is crosswise (right to left).

Into this classification fall the popular double knit, interlock knit, plain knit, rib knit, and purl knit. As these are further explained individually, you will probably recall instances when you questioned the meaning of each.

The double knit. As its name indicates, the double knit is attained by using two yarns and two sets of needles which interlock loops from opposite directions. It has great strength and can be relied upon not to run. Either side may be used as long as consistency is maintained, since both sides have the same rib-like look, with only slight variations. To determine the right side, cut a crosswise strip and stretch it. The edge of the material usually rolls to the right side. This fabric is a natural for dresses, slacks, jumpsuits, jackets, coats, and many other fashionable creations.

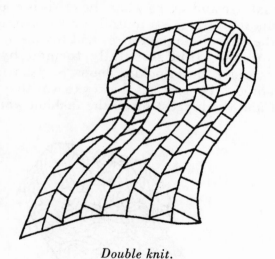

Double knit.

Interlock knit. A type of double knit the interlock knit is made by the same process and can be used similarly.

The rib knit. Distinguished by noticeable ridges, the rib knit is created by knit and purl stitches in the same row, thus allowing much crosswise stretch and close fit. This material is good for cardigans, pullovers, and vests.

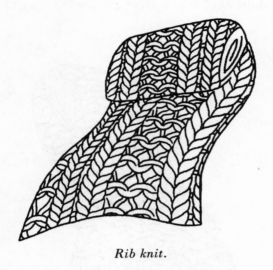

Rib knit.

The plain knit. As its name suggests, the plain knit has a knit front, that is, it is composed of the knit stitch only. The reverse side is an inverted knit stitch or purl stitch. Crosswise stretch is predominant, making it a choice for dresses, shells, jumpers, and slacks, just to mention a few.

Plain knit.

The purl knit. Recognizable, horizontal ridges of alternating knit and purl stitches identify the purl knit. This fabric has unusual lengthwise and crosswise stretch, with remarkable recoverability. This fabric is a wise choice for sports enthusiasts.

Purl knit.

Warp knits. Usually composed of two or more yarns in every loop, warp knits are produced by machine only, that is raschel and tricot. Their construction is more rigid than the weft knit, resulting in less stretch, and no run or sag. Great design variations (laces, stripes, plaids, etc.) are possible. Warp knits are distinguishable by straight edges.

The raschel knit. Of lace-like construction the raschel knit is created on the raschel knit machine. Although flimsy in appearance, the coarser yarn is stabilized by a finer yarn that limits its stretchability.

Tricot knit. Recognized by its fine crosswise rib which appears on the wrong side, tricot knit has more crosswise than vertical stretch, strength, and drapability. It is used most often in boudoir fashions such as lingerie and loungewear.

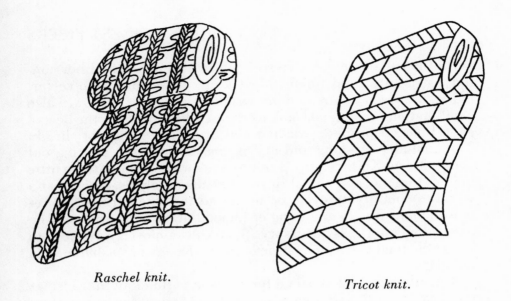

Raschel knit.

Tricot knit.

TO STRETCH OR NOT TO STRETCH

Although all knits stretch, some stretch more or less than others; that is why some are termed stable knits and others stretch knits.

Stable knits. Because of their moderate stretch (due to construction or bonding), stable knits are commonly used and easily recognized. (Bonding is the lamination of one or more layers of fabric, which gives stability.) Stable knits need not be stretched during pattern placement or sewing.

Stretch knits. Distinguishable by marked stretch and recovery, stretch knits are used for a close body fit. To determine the degree of stretch, refer to the stretch gauge on pattern envelopes. The stretch-knit fabric is sometimes cut with the knit in a stretched position; as might be the case when using a two-way stretch knit which has considerable stretch lengthwise and crosswise. When sewing, stretch slightly in front and in back of the stitching line. Read pattern instructions carefully for specific details.

Wise Sewers Know Their Knits.

Knit is usually a very carefree fabric because of its fiber content, structure, and finish. Most knits are made of polyester, nylon, or acrylic fibers and are wrinkle resistant. There are also combinations and blends of two or more fibers utilizing the best of each fiber. If properly washed and dried, they will not shrink. This includes washing and drying the fabric before cutting out your pattern. Knits require a gentle wash with warm water, a little mild detergent, and a cool rinse. It is absolutely essential that a warm-to-cool drying cycle be used and that the garment be removed *immediately* and hung or folded flat. A warm iron may be used if touching up is necessary. Wool knits almost always need to be dry cleaned unless the fabric is one of the newer washable wool blends.

A word of caution is called for here—a cotton knit may lose as much as four to six inches in washing and drying. A cotton-polyester combination will shrink less.

THE STRAIGHT STORY

Straightening a knit is not difficult. If the knit is tubular, first cut one fold open, and then press the other. With contrasting thread or chalk, mark across a horizontal rib from one edge to the other. Then also mark a vertical rib. These lines should form right

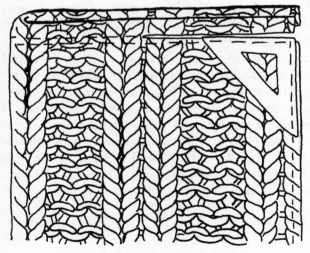

Straight grain.

angles when they meet. If they do not, the fabric must be straightened by an acceptable method, one of which is described below.

To straighten washable fabric, dampen the fabric well, and lay it on a flat surface. Using both hands, work the loop lines until they are perpendicular to the vertical ribs. Let dry. Steam press on the wrong side, maintaining the grain you have just achieved. You owe it to yourself to lay it on the line!

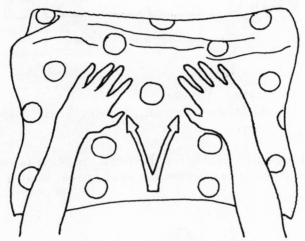

Method for straightening grain.

GET WHAT YOU'RE AFTER

The real worry in caring for a knit fabric—or any other fabric, for that matter—was eliminated by a federal law passed in 1972. It requires that all fabric manufacturers include a "care label" with each piece of fabric sold. Fiber content should, however, be checked to insure that the fabric being purchased will do what you want it to do. This information can be found on the end of the bolt or on a specially attached hang tag.

The following list contains familiar trademarks and the fibers of which they are made:

Fiber Content	*Trademarks*
Polyester	Dacron, Kodel, Fortrel, Trevira, Vycron
Acrylic	Acrilan, Orlon, Creslan, Sayelle, Zefran
Nylon	Antron, Qiana, Caprolan, Touch, Enkalure

Care labeling–a federal law.

Spandex	Lycra, Vyrene
Acetate	Celanese, Estron, Avisco, Acele, Celara
Triacetate	Arnel

Knit is the perfect fabric for the ideal outfit. It is easy to sew, comfortable to wear, and goes everywhere without a wrinkle.

2

Pick a Pattern

Some patterns can be used for both woven and knit fabrics. Others are for knits only and are marked accordingly on the pattern package. Still others specify for stretch knits only. Those patterns especially marked usually have eliminated darts and ease (the comfort allowance), and rely on the stretch of the knit to enhance fit.

Stretch-knit patterns have a gauge on the envelope to eliminate knits with insufficient stretch. There are patterns designed exclusively for knits which have many sizes included in each pattern envelope. These are especially useful for the hard-to-fit person. When using this type of pattern, measure all essential areas and draw them directly on the pattern. The pattern will then represent your exact body measurements—not those specified by the manufacturer. You can then cut out the pattern pieces, or draw them on superimposed thin paper or material which can be purchased for this purpose.

The advantage of the latter method is that if your body measurements change, you simple redraw and copy accordingly—no need for a new pattern. Patterns of this type can also be used for more than one person and still give a perfect fit every time. Patterns need not be complicated to make a fashion creation of distinctive elegance.

FACTS AND FIGURES

Basically, always consider five essential measurements before

25

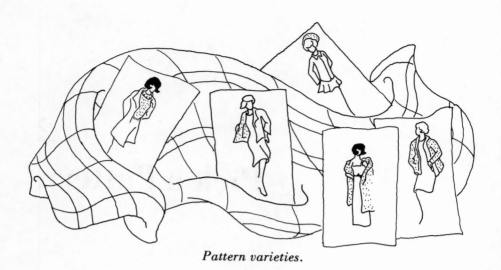

Pattern varieties.

choosing a pattern: bust, waist, hips, back neck to waist, and height. First, determine your figure type by comparing your height and back-waist length with the measurement chart in the back of the pattern book. This will put you in a definite figure type, so you can compare your body measurements with those on the chart. If you fall between two sizes and are small boned, choose the smaller. If you are large boned, choose the larger.

MEASURE WITH CARE

Measurements should be taken comfortably tight, and over the undergarments to be worn with the finished garment. Consult the following table for particulars.

Area to Be Measured	Procedure	Most Important for
Bust	Measure from fullest part of bust extending across back	Dresses, blouses, and jackets
Waist	Measure natural waistline or smallest portion of waist	Skirts, pants, dresses
Hips	Measure over fullest part of hips, seven to nine inches from natural waistline	Pants, skirts, dresses, and jumpsuits
Back Waist Length	Measure from prominent bone at base of neck to natural waistline	Dresses, jackets, and some blouses

Crotch Length	Take while seated on a flat surface. Measure from side of natural waist to flat surface	Pants and jumpsuits
Thigh	Measure fullest portion of upper leg.	Pants and jumpsuits
Outside Leg	Measure from waist to desired finished length	Pants and jumpsuits
Shoulder	Measure from neck base to top of arm	Dresses, blouses, and jackets
Arm	With arm at a right angle, measure from top to wristbone.	Dress, blouse and jacket sleeve lengths

Shape up your assets with complete, correct, and accurate measurements.

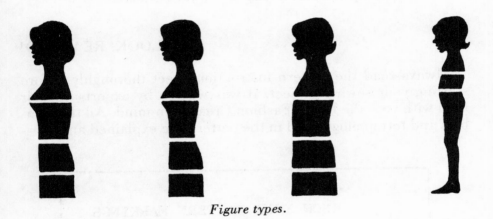

Figure types.

METRIC MEASUREMENTS

Since most patterns and sewing equipment include metric measurements, it is worthwhile to consider a few pertinent principles here.

In the metric system, one basic unit represents each area of measurement. In measuring length a meter is used which is slightly longer than a yard (39.37 inches). To this basic unit (meter) prefixes, representing powers of 10, can be added. Pertinent prefixes are:

deci	meaning	1/10
centi	meaning	1/100
milli	meaning	1/1000

By combining the basic unit in measuring length (meter) with the afore mentioned prefixes, you can arrive at the units of measurement most frequently encountered in sewing.

decimeter (dm)	1/10 of a meter
centimeter (cm)	1/100 of a meter
millimeter (mm)	1/1000 of a meter

If your waist measures 61 cm (24 inches), you can also interpret it as: .61 meters or 6.1 decimeters. It is easier to learn the metric units and what they represent than to convert them to inches, feet, and yards. If you learn essential metric units, you have only a minimal amount of conversion to do between systems. Should you wish to refer to a conversion chart, a table of metric-english equivalents is listed below.

1 cm equals 0.39 inch	1 inch equals 2.54 cm
1 m equals 3.28 feet	1 foot equals 0.305 m
1 m equals 1.09 yards	1 yard equals 0.91 m

LOOK! READ! DO!

Always read the pattern instruction sheet thoroughly before starting your sewing project. It was written by experts in their field with you, the Home Fashion Creator, in mind. All the symbols and terminology used in the pattern are explained and illus-

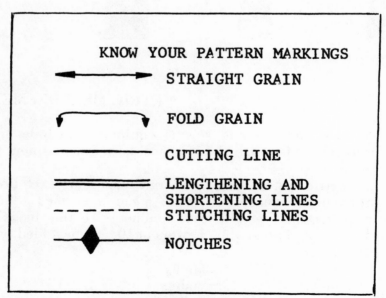

Pattern symbols explained.

trated clearly. This sheet takes you step-by-step, in an organized manner, through your sewing project. Explicit descriptions, detailed illustrations, and professional information offered are sure to make you a more proficient, confident Home Fashion Creator.

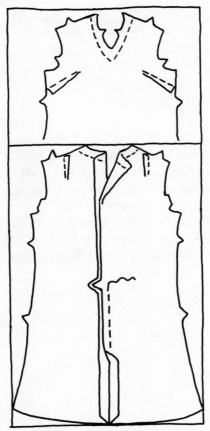

Top: Neck staystitching and bust darts. Bottom: Shoulder darts and center-back seam.

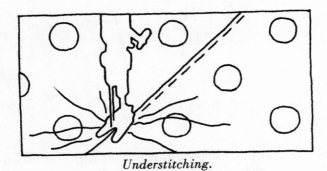

Understitching.

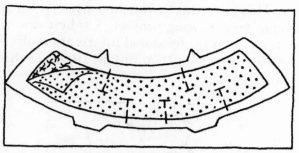
Collar interfacing.

PATTERN ALTERATIONS

Altering a pattern means personalizing it to your specific figure proportions. Compare your basic body measurements with those on the pattern envelope. If they differ at all, you will have to change the pattern accordingly.

Lengthening and shortening. The most common pattern alterations are also the two easiest—lengthening and shortening. Most patterns have lengthening and shortening lines for this purpose.

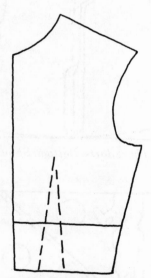
Bodice adjustment line.

To shorten, fold out necessary amount along indicated line in area concerned. To lengthen, cut along lengthening line, add paper

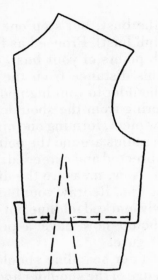

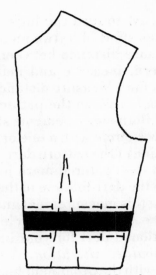

Bodice adjustment: Fold to shorten.   *Bodice adjustment: Add to lengthen.*

strip of the required amount behind the pattern, and tape. Remember to do the same thing on both pattern back and front.

Alteration of bust dart. In a dress, blouse or jacket, the bust dart is the most detailed to change. Choose the pattern size closest to your bust measurement, then determine if the darts are positioned properly for you. The point of the dart should be

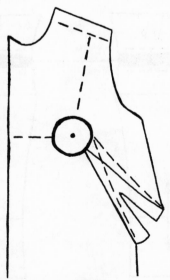

Repositioned bust dart.

31

directed toward the high point of the bust, but stop one or two inches short of it (two inches for a full bust). Proceed as follows: measure distance between the high points of your bust. On the pattern, measure and mark half this distance from the center front line. Measure distance from shoulder to your high point and indicate this on the pattern, measuring from the shoulder seam line. Both measurements should now meet, forming one marking. Draw a circle with a one or two-inch radius around the point. The foldline of the pattern dart, when redirected and extended, should meet the centered mark just drawn. Now, measure the distance from the dart-foldline to the stitching line. Redraw your bust dart, using this measurement and the newly marked foldline but ending at the edge of the circle. You should now have a perfectly positioned dart for your individual figure.

Shoulder alteration. A set-in shoulder seamline should coincide with the prominent bone at the edge of the shoulder and top of the arm. Lengthen or shorten shoulder area accordingly. If neck-to-waist measurement differs from that on the pattern, adjust according to paragraph 2 of this chapter.

Pant and jumpsuit alterations. Adjustments in pants and jumpsuits need not be complicated. Take a crotch measurement while seated on a flat surface, from natural waist to flat surface. Compare with crotch measurement on pattern and adjust if necessary. Lengthen or shorten legs on lines indicated (paragraph 2 of this chapter). If thigh area is too tight, increase by adding equal

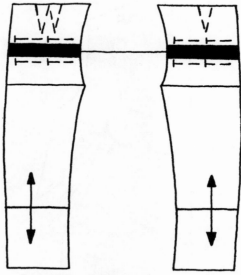

Pant adjustment: Lengthen crotch.

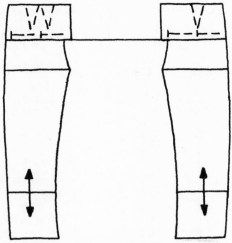

Pant adjustment: Shorten crotch.

amounts to thigh seam areas. If too loose, diminish by taking equal amounts from each seam area. If hip or lower leg area needs adjusting, follow same procedures.

Skirt alterations. To increase hip area of a skirt, add equal amounts to front and back side seams. If fullness is concentrated in the front, add only to front seams. If fullness is concentrated in back, add to back seams. If waistline is too small, lengthen

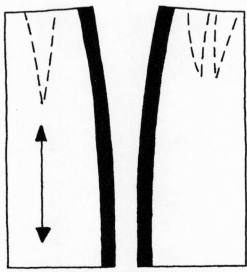

Skirt adjustment: Increase hip area.

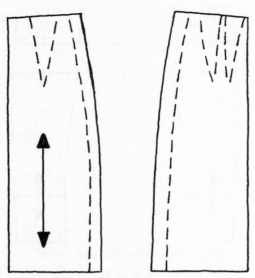

Skirt adjustment: Decrease hip area.

waistband the necessary amount, adding proportionately to the upper skirt side seam. If waistline is too large, decrease waistband.

To insure a perfect fit with each new pattern, take a little extra time to make an unadorned, inexpensive copy. Doing so is time well spent. Necessary changes are readily seen, and can be adapted to the pattern for a fashion-smart creation.

3

Quality Tools, Not Quantity

Time and money spent on proper sewing accessories will reflect in a professionally finished garment and a happier, more confident "You." The quality of your tools definitely counts too. For that reason, the following list has been compiled especially for knits and found to be workably successful.

Fabric shears. From seven to nine inches long, fabric shears especially made for knits, will make cutting a pleasant part of your sewing project. Some have a precision-ground knife-edge, some are serrated, and some are stainless steel, especially light in weight and very sharp. A pair of inexpensive shears is a poor investment, but one made of steel (especially by the hot-dropped forged method) will maintain its sharpness and give lasting satisfaction. For serviceability, speed, and ease of operation, electric

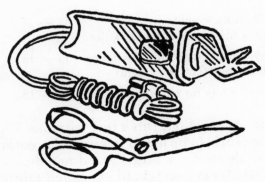

Electric scissors and fabric shears.

scissors also help to produce a clean-cut garment. A pair of snipping scissors, which is a palm-sized cutting instrument, is handy for snipping loose threads.

Ballpoint pins and needles. Especially designed to be used on knit fabrics, the rounded points of ballpoint pins and needles gently push fabric yarn aside rather than piercing or breaking it. Always keep needles in assorted sizes on hand for fabrics of varying weights. A new needle will eliminate snags and skipped stitches. An appropriate stitch length is 12-15 stitches per inch and should be used on each new garment.

Pin cushion with ballpoint pins and needles.

Correct needle size is essential for good workmanship. A needle that is too fine for the fabric will bend or break. A needle that is too thick will leave a distorted stitching line. This can be evidenced by the perforation about each stitch. In some instances, a run in the knit might even occur. To eliminate these potential problems, refer to the following chart.

Type of Knit	Needle Size	
Delicate: Warp knits including tricot or jersey	9 or	70
Top weight: single knits including tricot, jersey, cotton, and cotton polyester combinations	9 — 11	70 — 80
Light weight to Medium weight: weft knits including 6½-8 ounce double knits	11 — 14	80 — 90
Medium to Heavy weight: weft knits including 10-12 ounce double knits (bottom weight)	14 — 16	90 — 100
Extra Heavy — weft knits for outerwear	16 — 18	100 — 110

For complete satisfaction, run a test stitching line on a double thickness of the fabric to be used. In areas of greater thickness, it might be advisable to use a larger sized needle.

Fabric weights. Heavy metal cubes, called fabric weights can be used in place of ballpoint pins and are great time-savers.

Fabric weight.

Approximately six weights will do an adequate job of holding pattern and material in place until cut.

Adhesive spray. Another time-saver for pattern placement without pins is an adhesive spray. When sprayed on pattern pieces, the pieces will adhere gently to the material and allow a perfect cut. This clinging ability will remain throughout several cuttings. Of course, manufacturer's instructions must always be followed carefully.

Tailor's chalk. A quick, convenient method of marking, tailor's chalk comes in a variety of colors. Little scraps of hand and bath soap, those bathroom rejects, do the same job with no worry of show-through. Both are very satisfactory methods.

Tracing paper and wheel. Pattern symbols can also be transferred by using tracing paper and wheel. Read directions on the package very carefully.

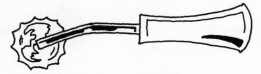

Tracing wheel.

Tape measure. By all means purchase a good sixty-inch tape measure that won't stretch or shrink. Although a cloth or plastic measuring tape may do either, it is a better purchase than the spring type, which can be temperamental.

Sixty-inch tape measure.

Other accessories. A wrist pin cushion is convenient to use and will leave both hands free for measuring and pinning. A *sewing gauge* is a small six-inch measure which can be used to mark precise details. A *seam ripper* will eliminate those few inevitable mistakes with little lost time or effort. *Beeswax or paraffin*, used by our grandmothers for adding strength and durability to thread (especially for buttons), still has no substitute. *Double-faced zipper tape or transparent tape* is helpful in zipper applications. Transparent tape also can be used for quick marking, topstitching, buttonhole indication, and stabilizing.

Wrist pin cushion.

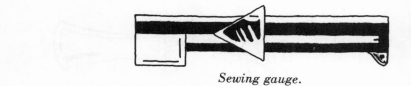

Sewing gauge.

Seam ripper.

Beeswax.

Your choice of thread will depend on the fiber content and fabric color to be used. The following rules apply. If fabric content is entirely or mainly synthetic (e.g., polyester, nylon, or acrylic), a synthetic thread such as 100% polyester or a cotton-wrapped polyester core thread, should be selected. Each has the necessary stretch, strength, and compatible care characteristics. Be aware, however, that cotton-wrapped thread may have a tendency to unravel, causing a ball of cotton fuzz to form at the needle tip. This, of course, necessitates cutting and rethreading.

If the knit is of animal origin, such as wool, use silk thread which is elastic, lustrous, and strong. It stretches, permanently molds with the fabric, and produces an even, flat, unpuckered seam.

A thread stemming from plant life, such as the cotton-wrapped polyester core, can be used more compatibly with a cotton knit. Another synthetic thread made of fine nylon-bonded filaments is the recommended choice for fabrics which require extreme stretch and strength, such as those used in ski wear and lingerie. Now available is a staple synthetic thread made from short polyester fiber lengths rather than the filament construction normally used to manufacture synthetic thread. Though it is 100% polyester, it sews with the ease of cotton due to its similarity in construction.

Zippers, trims, and elastic should also be compatible with the fashion fabric being used. They are available in polyester and nylon. All are light weight, flexible, and suitable for most knits.

4

The Inside Story

Do you want your garment to have the same smooth, controlled appearance of ready-to-wear? Then special consideration should be given to linings and interfacings. They are out of sight but should not be out of mind. *Interfacing.* A third layer of fabric applied between a facing and outer fabric is called interfacing. It is used for shaping, supporting, and stabilizing. It can be woven, non-woven, or fusible, and should not be heavier than the outer shell to which it is attached. Draping interfacing together with fabric over your hand is a good test of whether they will combine well or not. Woven interfacing has grain and therefore must be cut on grain. Non-woven interfacing does not have grain and can be cut in any direction, making even small scraps usable. Fusible interfacing is heat-sensitive and is applied between two layers of fabric if adhesive on both sides, or directly to the wrong side of the

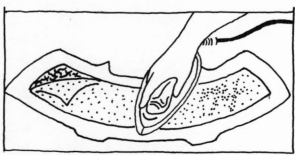

Heat-sensitive interfacing.

fabric if only one side is fusible. It is especially useful for small areas and eliminates the need for padding stitches.

Lining. Another shaping material is lining. It is sewn separately and then joined to the outer garment at major points. It gives a finished appearance to the inside of a garment. Lining is quite often omitted in knits because it inhibits the stretch and drapability of the fabric. Seams can be finished attractively with either a knit or zigzag stitch. If lining is desired, a lightweight knit lining or fabric such as tricot will curtail the freedom of the outer fabric only slightly. Both interfacing and lining, if used, should have the same properties as the fashion fabric. Therefore, if your knit is washable, so too should be your lining and interfacing. Pattern envelopes indicate amounts needed.

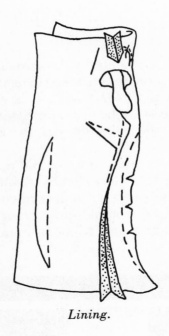

Lining.

5

Before You Cut

Pattern placement is essentially the same for knits as for woven fabric. In knit fabrics, the lengthwise rib or wale is comparable to the lengthwise grain of woven fabric. It is your guide to placing pattern pieces on the straight of grain. Straight-grain indicators on pattern pieces should coincide with the lengthwise rib of the fabric.

Should the knit be tubular, cut one fold open, press the other, and place right sides together. Plaids, stripes, and one-way designs are handled differently (as is described below). Now you're ready to start pattern placement—presuming, of course, that you have prepared the fabric according to manufacturer's instruc-

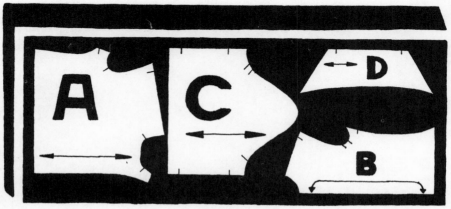

Proper pattern placement.

tions, straightened ribs if necessary, and indicated needed alterations. Because of slight shading some knits should be cut all in one direction. In tubular knit, very often the fold crease can not be pressed out, so do not center pattern pieces on it. Check for any such conditions.

Observe the layout suggestions for the desired view and width of your fabric. Velours and furs are cut in one direction using a with-nap layout. Plaids, stripes, and one-way designs are usually cut from single fabric, with the right side up for easier matching. Reverse pattern pieces and match carefully when cutting a second piece.

Fasten the pattern to the fashion fabric, mark according to your preference, then cut. When cutting, use sharp fabric shears to make long strokes, and keep material as close as possible to the flat surface on which you're cutting. A poor cut can lead only to a poor fit. Remember to cut notches out, not off.

A cutting board, found in most fabric or notions departments, can be helpful in laying out your pattern. It is measured off in inches, and also has bias markings. Short, tack-like pins can be purchased for use with this cutting aid.

MARKSMANSHIP

Knits can be marked with any of the standard methods employed for woven fabrics, plus a few new ones. In any method, the aim is perfect marksmanship. The structure and stability of the knit will determine the most favorable method. Some are better than others; some are quick and easy. The choice is yours. However, it is a good idea to experiment first with a scrap of the knit to be used. This will quickly eliminate ineffective methods.

Tailor's chalk. Tailor's chalk comes in a limited assortment of colored and white squares and, if applied lightly, is removed easily by laundering. It works well on hard surfaced, stable knits and is less effective, but visible on softer knits. Choose a contrasting color.

With a pin, gently scratch out the tissue surface of the symbol to be transferred. Then place one square of chalk underneath the bottom layer of fabric and directly beneath the symbol to be transferred. With another square of chalk, mark through the tissue with a gentle, rubbing stroke. The chalk in hand marks the top fabric. The gentle, rubbing action on the bottom chalk marks the second layer. Thus, two layers of fabric are marked simultaneously.

Soap. Small pieces of soap, bathroom-reject size, are ideal for marking all knits except white. The soap must be dry; not soft and moist. Soap can be used effectively on both hard and soft-surfaced knits, and can be applied in the same manner as tailor's chalk. An additional advantage of soap is that is will launder out easily in the first washing. You will find however, that most often steam pressing completely eliminates it.

Tracing paper and wheel. Necessary markings on hard-surfaced, stable knits can be produced by using tracing paper and wheel. Insert tracing paper above the upper and beneath the lower fabric, with carbon side to the fabric. Press the wheel over the markings to be transferred. This pressure should transfer the colored markings to the fabric. Quite often, however, the pressure required may cut the pattern; and a color dark enough to show up is difficult to get out. For this method of marking, read manufacturer's instructions carefully. Remember when marking, only *you* have to see and understand the markings, so develop a light touch.

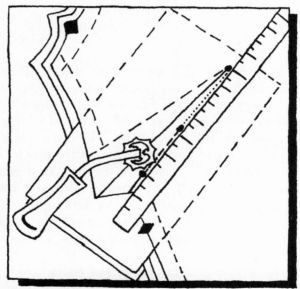

Transfer of markings with tracing paper and wheel.

Tailor's tacks. These are thread symbols that can be used to mark all types of knits, but especially soft, springy types. Tailor's tacks are made as follows: with an unknotted double strand of thread (in a slightly different color from the fabric) make a small stitch through the tissue and both fabric layers then, make another stitch over the first, pulling to form a loop. Leave a loose connecting thread and continue procedure on next symbol if it is reasonably close. When marking is complete, cut the loops and connecting threads, then remove the tissue. Carefully separate the fabric layers and cut the connecting threads. Tiny tufts result at each desired spot.

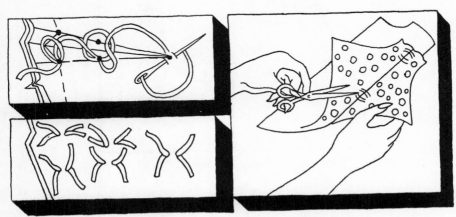

Tailor's tacks: Step 1, above left; step 2, below left; step 3, right.

Transparent tape. A quick way to mark such symbols as darts, buttonholes, pockets, and applique placement is with transparent tape. For darts, fold the tissue back along one side of the dart. Then apply the tape directly to the fabric underneath the dart line to be transferred. Repeat the process on the remaining layer of fabric.

Symbols to be transferred to pattern pieces include the following:

1. O's (small and large). The necessity of each can be found on the pattern instruction sheet.

2. Button and buttonhole markings. These indicate placement of buttons and buttonholes and suggested lengths of buttonholes.

3. Centers and foldlines. These indicators are essential for perfect construction and fit.

4. Darts. The ultimate purpose of darts is to achieve a good fit; however with knit fabrics this is often unnecessary.

5. Placement lines. These positioning lines indicate placement of pockets, pleats, and some trims.

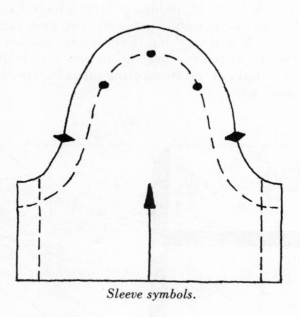

Sleeve symbols.

Buttonhole and center-line symbols.

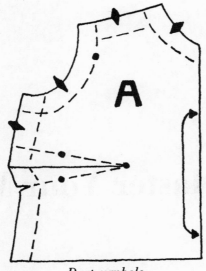

Dart symbols.

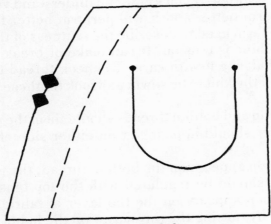

Pocket symbols.

6
Master Your Machine

Getting to know your machine fully may be a wonderful new experience for you. Read your machine manual carefully to acquaint yourself with all your machine's precision features and available accessories. If you know and understand your machine, you will perform better and it will perform better for you.

Tension. A term used to describe the tautness of thread used in a sewing machine is tension. It can make or break your fashion creation, so balance it with care. To check thread tension use a folded scrap of the knit to be sewn, and look for these particulars:

• The top and bobbin threads should tie in the middle of the fabric. Neither should appear flat on either side of the layered fabric.

• If a loop appears on the bottom thread, the top tension is too loose and should be regulated with the top tension knob.

• If a loop appears on the top layer of fabric, tighten the lower tension by turning the tiny screw on the bobbin case to the right, a little at a time.

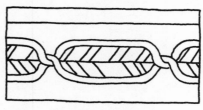

Balanced tension.

In addition to the above, always use thread of the same consistency in both needle and bobbin. Never fill a bobbin over old thread.

Use a new ballpoint needle, compatible in size with the weight of the knit being used, for each new garment. (Refer to needle chart.) These pointers will help eliminate possible snags and skipped stitches. Clean your machine with a machine brush after each garment is completed. Lint accumulates quickly when knits are sewn, and is quite abrasive.

Stitch selection. Will depend on the type of machine used. If your machine is a newer model, with knit stitches on it, you can choose from a variety of ideal stretch stitches. If it is a zigzag model, use a zigzag stitch, small to medium size. (A zigzag stitch is a less sophisticated stretch stitch.) If your machine is a straight-stitch machine, use twelve to fifteen stitches per inch for stretch knits, and stretch the knit slightly in front and back of the stitch as you sew. When using a straight stitch, sew a double row of stitches to insure against broken seams, especially in stress areas such as crotch and underarm.

No matter what type machine you're using, always start stitching with long upper and lower threads pulled to the back of the presser foot. Hold threads taut until the stitched fabric is about an inch behind the presser foot. Using this procedure, knotting at the throat plate can usually be avoided. A throat plate with a small opening also helps to eliminate snarls.

For general-purpose sewing, a hinged presser foot or roller foot will accommodate various knit thicknesses. For specialty stitching, refer to your manual for correct attachments and other particulars.

7
Pressing

Pressing is an indispensable skill which all Home Fashion Creators will want to perform with perfection. Pressing does matter. It is the secret ingredient that can make a fashion creation mediocre, or a magnificent achievement in the world of high fashion.

Pointers on Pressing Knits. To press proceed as follows: Use an iron setting appropriate for the fabric being pressed. With a single motion, place the iron on the desired area and let the heat penetrate. Then lift the iron and place it on the next area to be pressed. Do not glide the iron from one area to the next; as this distorts the grain and causes ripples in the fabric which often cannot be removed.

Most pressing is done on the wrong side of the fabric, with or without a press cloth. For a soft press, that is, one you might want to remove, use a heated iron without steam. To hard press, or set a press, use steam. Always test the iron on an inconspicuous portion of the garment to make sure the heat is on the proper setting and will not damage the fabric. Also note if a shine appears on the right side of fabric. If the setting is appropriate and a shine does not appear, you need not use a press cloth. If a shine does appear, it will be necessary to use a press cloth. You can purchase a press cloth or drill cloth in a notions department or a fabric shop. A double or triple layer of nylon net makes an excellent press cloth because steam penetrates the fabric easily and will not cause a shine.

Structural seams should be pressed open if stitched with a

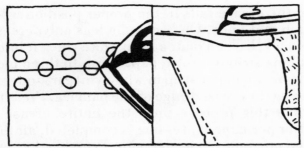
Left: Structured seam. Right: Bust and elbow darts.

Sleeve seam on sleeve board.   *Curved area on pressing ham.*

straight or zigzag stitch. If stitched with a knit stitch, press them to one side or the other. Press bust and elbow darts downward, and shoulder and waistline darts toward the center. Any portion of a garment which will be worn over a curved area of the body should be pressed over a curved area. A pressing ham and seam roll are appropriate for these areas. In an emergency, a fluffed-up terry towel can be substituted.

Press continuously, as the garment is being constructed. Never stitch one seam or dart to another before pressing. Pressing during construction assures accurate placement and fit and eliminates what some call a homemade look.

After completing a garment, press it again, carefully. If it is a stable knit, hang it on a padded hanger. If it is a stretchable knit, do not hang the garment, but lay it carefully in a drawer or chest.

PERMANENT PRESSING

Before permanently pressing a crease in pants, always press the crease by the soft-press method and try on the pants to make certain that the crease falls in the proper position which is normally through mid-knee. On back pant legs only, creases extend just to crotch level. Then pour a little white vinegar into a shallow dish. Cut a long strip of brown paper, two to three inches wide. Immerse the brown paper strip in white vinegar, squeeze loosely, and place along the creased edge of one pant leg. Press paper until dry. Continue this process until the entire crease has been pressed. After permanent pressing is completed, air the garment for a few hours to remove vinegar odor. Pressing, like stitching, is always done in the direction of the grain.

USEFUL PRESSING ACCESSORIES AND SUBSTITUTES

A *tailor's ham* can be purchased or made quite simply. Make a small, circular pillow about the size of an average hand from a wool, polyester, or other scrap, leaving one small portion open. Pack tightly with sawdust, nylons, cotton or dacron batting. Sawdust is best because it holds heat and packs tightly. Stitch opening.

A *seam roll* is similar to a tailor's ham except that it is longer and narrower. It can be purchased or made by carefully and tightly rolling a terry towel.

A *sleeve board* is a miniature ironing board useful in pressing sleeve seams. Again, a rolled terry towel may be substituted.

A *trailer ironing board* is a small, tabletop ironing board, useful for pressing flat areas of garments.

A *point presser* looks like a very tiny, unpadded sleeve board except that the upper edge has a thin, pointed area and the lower edge, a wider, pointed area. Cardboard cut to a specific point may be substituted.

A *needle board* is a small board with tiny projections to accommodate napped fabric. A piece of self fabric or terry cloth is a good substitute.

Part II

8
Let's Put It All Together

The beautiful knit wardrobe you hope to make will become an enviable reality if you also learn and practice the knit sewing techniques in this chapter. In some instances, the techniques vary only slightly from those of woven fabric, while others will be unique to knits alone.

The alphabetized presentation of terms and technology is convenient, concise, and clearly illustrated. Just Between the Two of Us will supply you with enough helpful hints to avoid many sewing frustrations. The following fabric key is provided to further simplify your understanding of the illustrated material.

Key to Illustrations:

right side	wrong side	lining	interfacing

Appliqué. An appliqué is a decorative design or figure made of fabric and sewn to a fabric background. To fasten appliqué to fabric, proceed as follows: first hold appliqué in place with pins or transparent tape. Then use a straight or zigzag stitch to secure it and then a shorter zigzag or decorative stitch to finish its contours. A raised outline can be achieved by sewing over gimp (a very narrow cord). Adjust the stitch length so that the fabric feeds smoothly.

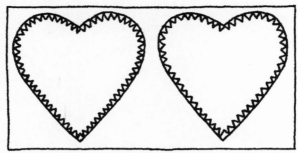

Appliqué.

Belt. To make a tie belt, proceed as follows: Cut a lengthwise strip of fabric equal to the waist measurement (or hip measurement for hip belt) plus desired length for tie ends and seam allowances. (The width should equal twice the width desired plus seam allowances). Then fold fabric lengthwise, right sides together, and stitch, leaving an opening in the center. Grade or bevel seams, turn, and press. Slipstitch the opening.

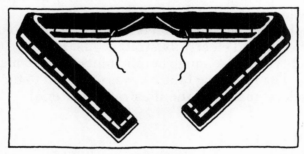

Tie belt.

To make a string or tube belt proceed as follows: Cut a lengthwise strip of fabric equal to the waist or hip measurement plus desired length for tie ends and seam allowances. (Width should equal twice the width of cording used plus seam allowance). Then insert gimp between right sides of material, keeping edges even. Sew across top and along edges, leaving enough room to turn. Do not trim seam allowance. Pull cording through tube, turning belt to the right side. (The seam allowance will compensate for the loss of cording). Cut off cording, slipstitch, and knot ends.

Bevel. Bevel is a term used to describe cutting one or more layers of fabric on an inclination or slope. It is a cutting technique used to eliminate bulk in seams. It can be used in place of layering or grading. When beveling, hold shears at an extreme angle and cut through all seams at once. This should result in seams at various inclinations or slants.

Button. A button is a fastener used to hold two parts of a garment together. It is placed at a point of stress and is held in position with a double strand of thread, yarn, or a metal toggle. Drawing the thread through beeswax or paraffin strengthens it and eliminates many lost buttons. Most buttons have a projection on the back called a shank to glide the button smoothly through the buttonhole. A similar projection can be created with thread as the button is sewn. Snap-on buttons and button molds for self-fabric are available with illustrated instructions. To avoid gapping in a jacket or dress, place the first two buttons at the waist and bust with the others an equal distance apart. Allow approximately one-half inch between button and outer edge of garment. The size of a button determines its buttonhole length, so purchase buttons in advance of buttonholing.

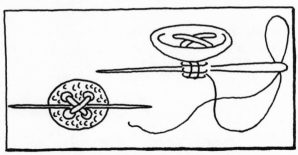

Button.

Buttonhole (machine-made). Mark proper position with chalk, tiny soap scrap, tape or contrasting thread. The size of the buttonhole should equal diameter of button plus thickness plus ⅛ inch. To determine this measurement tie a piece of yarn around the button. Half of it plus ⅛ inch equals the buttonhole length. A buttonhole in knit fabric is better sewn lengthwise for less stretching and with a zigzag stitch to avoid puckering.

Corded buttonholes. A buttonhole recommended for knits, made by sewing over a heavy thread or gimp loop is called a

57

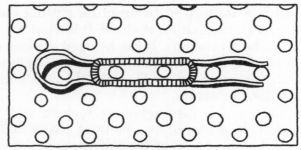
Corded buttonhole.

corded buttonhole. Some buttonhole feet have a projection at the rear for holding thread or gimp in this type buttonhole. Sew buttonhole as usual, but direct stitching over the heavy thread or gimp. When finished, pull the loose ends of thread to one end of the buttonhole with the loop reinforcing the other end. Thread the loose ends through a needle, work to the reverse side, and knot.

Machine buttonholes are made through interfacing and facing. The buttonhole procedure can be accomplished easily on a sweater knit by sewing through a piece of transparent tape at the buttonhole location. Upon completion, the tape is then pulled away.

Bound buttonholes are a smart addition to a stable knit. They are made through interfacing, but not facing. Proceed as follows:

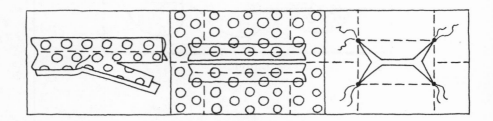

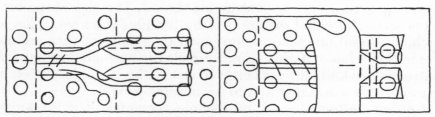
Bound buttonholes: Strip method.

Fold a long one-inch strip of fabric lengthwise, wrong sides together. Stitch ⅛ inch from fold and trim to ¼ inch. Cut into strips one inch longer than buttonhole. On right side of garment, pin and center raw edge of strip to buttonhole line. Stitch over previous stitching line, the *exact* length of buttonhole line, then do same on the other side of the buttonhole line. On the wrong side cut between stitching, as illustrated. Turn strips to the inside, baste outside closed. Turn outside back, exposing strip ends and triangle. Stitch triangle to strip ends, as illustrated. Press.

A quick way to finish the facing side is to stitch in the ditch (depression) around the buttonhole, on the outside of the garment. On the inside of the garment, trim out facing very close to the stitching line. This two-piece strip method of making bound buttonholes on knit is easier and more accurate than the patch, or so-called window pane, method.

Casing. A casing is a tunnel of fabric through which elastic or other drawstring can be drawn to enhance fit. It is sewn top and bottom on the wrong side of the fabric. Sometimes a buttonhole is made where the drawstring enters and exits.

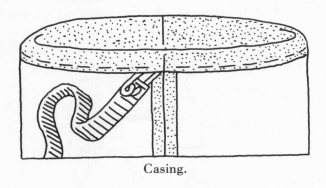

Casing.

Clip. A clip is a small scissors cut within the seam allowance.

Collar. A collar, consists of an upper collar and a lower collar and serves as a finish or accent to a garment. It can be sewn to the neckline or can serve as a separate unit to put on or take off as you wish. Collar shapes vary. Proceed as follows: Sew right sides together, leaving neckline edge open. Grade or bevel seams and clip curves. Turn collar and press with outer seam rolled to the underside of collar. Collar is then attached, right side up, to the neckline. For a separate collar the seamline is continued around the neckline edge, leaving a few inches open for turning. Trim,

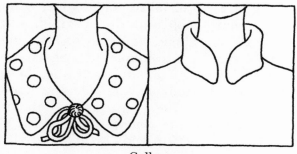

Collars.

clip curves and press as above. Slipstitch the opening.

If more body is desired, interfacing may be used. If woven or non-woven interfacing is used, sew it to the under collar. Press-on interfacing works well on knits and is applied to the upper collar. For proper application, follow manufacturer's instructions.

Cuff. A cuff is a shaped piece of fabric used as a finish or trim on a sleeve or pant leg. For sleeve application, follow same general instructions as for collar but attach to sleeve lower edge. For a pant leg, a mock —*french cuff* is quick to do and results in a neat finish. A *conventional cuff* can also be used on a pant leg.

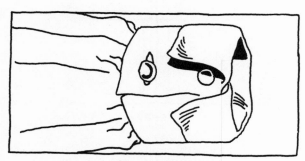

Sleeve cuff.

For a mock-french cuff proceed as follows: at bottom of pant leg turn under desired cuff width to the wrong side, then turn over again. Stitch approximately a ¼-inch seam around upper edge of turned fabric through pant leg. Drop remainder of turned allowance down. Press with ¼ inch seam turned upward.

For a conventional cuff, proceed as follows: Sew pants seams to within 3½ times the desired cuff depth. Clip seam at finishing

60

Conventional cuff.

point and press. Turn to right side, fold under 1½ times desired cuff depth, seam, trim, and press. The unattached under edge may be sewn by machine, with a zigzag or straight stitch, or slipstitched by hand. After turning up cuff, you may wish to stitch in the ditch (seam depression) or make a few inconspicuous stitches in the side seams to hold cuff in place.

Dart. A dart is a stitched tapering fold used to achieve good fit, but often unnecessary in knits, especially stretch knits. Follow specified pattern markings and sew from wide to narrow, securing ends. Press bust and elbow darts downwards, others to the center. If fabric is very bulky, darts may be cut to within ¼ inch of the point and pressed open.

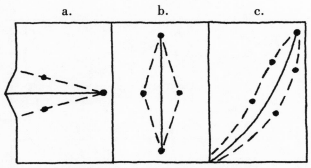

Types of darts: a. Straight dart, b. Double-pointed dart, c. French dart.

Directional stitching. Stitching with the grain, called directional stitching, prevents seams from stretching and helps to maintain proper grain lines. To determine direction of grain, run hand along an edge of the material. (Remove selvage if necessary). If the edge remains smooth, you are rubbing with the grain. If it frays, you are rubbing against the grain.

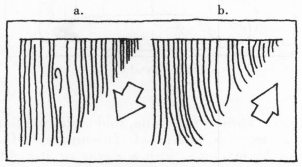

Fabric grain: a. With grain. b. Against grain.

Edgestitching. Used to retard raveling, edge stitching consists of a line of stitches, either straight, zigzag, or knit, along the edge of a seam or seam allowance. Most knits do not have a tendency to ravel, thus making edgestitching unnecessary. Edgestitching can also be done on the outside of a garment, as a row of machine-regulation stitches very close to an edge.

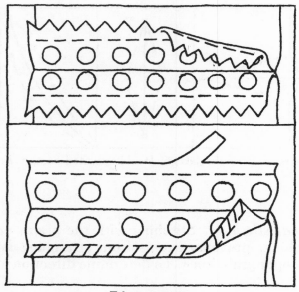

Edgestitching.

Facing. Facing is a shaped piece of fabric used as an edge finish primarily for necklines and armholes. To face, proceed as follows: Stitch right side of facing to right side of desired edge. Understitch facing to seam allowance close to seamline, clip, and trim seams. Press toward facing. At shoulder seams or other areas where stitches can be hidden, handstitch to inside seam allowance of garment.

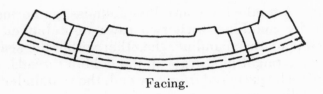

Facing.

Flap. A flap is a piece of fabric sewn to or above a pocket as a decorative accent and is usually interfaced. To prepare and attach a flap proceed as follows: Using a predetermined piece of fabric (right sides together), make a crosswise fold and stitch sides. Bevel seamed edges and clip if necessary. Turn and press, rolling seams slightly to underside. Attach by placing seamline, raw edges facing downward, on indicated garment placement line, and stitch. Trim lower layer of seams. Turn upper seam allowance over lower, making diagonal folds at corners to encase raw edges. Stitch and press.

Pocket flap.

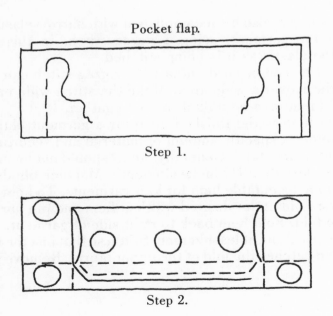

Step 1.

Step 2.

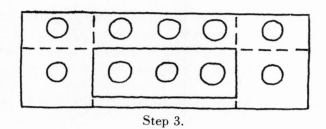

Step 3.

Gathering. A method of controlling fullness, gathering is done effectively by machine with two rows of unlocked basting stitches— one on the seamline, the other within the seam allowance. With a straight pin, draw up the bobbin threads. Pull half the distance to be gathered from one end, the remainder from the other end. Adjust and secure threads.

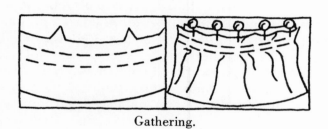

Gathering.

Gathering can also be accomplished with narrow elastic on the inside of the garment, using a zigzag stitch. In this method, stretch the elastic as it is being stitched.

A heavy thread or cord and a wide zigzag stitch can produce even gathers over a wide area. Make the stitch wide enough so that the thread can be pulled freely to gather.

Hem. A hem is the finished edge for a garment obtained by turning under a specific amount of material and securing it with stitches or fusible tape. Generally, hems should not be more than 3 inches or less than 1½ inches in depth. Machine blindstitching produces an acceptable hem for knit garments. To hem proceed as follows: Fold under desired width of hem and pin horizontally along the fold. Fold hem back to right side of garment, allowing hem edge to extend at least ¼ inch. Stitch so that just the tip of the blindstitch catches the fold of the upper fabric. Remove pins and press.

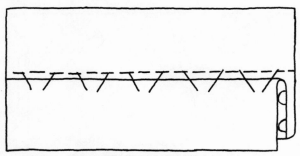

Blindstitch hem.

It is not necessary to clean-finish a knit hem. Most knits do not ravel, and the turned-under edge would create extra bulk with no practical benefit. If a more finished look is desired, a knit or zigzag stitch can be used on the raw edge of the hem. Prewashed stretch lace and bias tape can also be added for a couture look.

For a circular or full skirt, use a gathering thread to control fullness before stitching. A heat-sensitive, fusible hemming tape, used according to manufacturer's instructions, will produce an attractive, flexible hem on stable, lightweight knits. It is both washable and dry cleanable.

To catchstitch a hem, proceed as above, using the stitch illustrated in place of the blindstitch. Because it gives with the fabric, this is a good hand-stitched hem for knits.

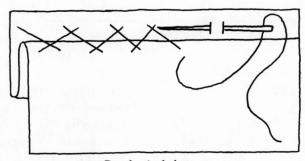

Catchstitch hem.

A tailor's hem is achieved by positioning the fabric in a like manner, but securing with a hand blindstitch as illustrated, then pressing. This type of hem is most often used with heavier fabric.

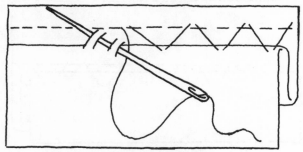

Tailor's hem.

To lockstitch a hem, work from left to right. Secure a stitch in the hem, then a shallow stitch in the garment. Make another stitch in the garment and hem together, directing needle through loop as illustrated. Press. All handstitched hems are sewn with a single thread.

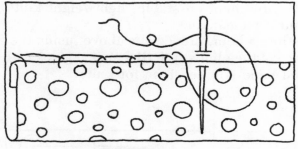

Lockstitch hem.

Hook and eye. A hook and eye is a two-part fastener often used on necklines, belts, and waistlines to fasten overlapping edges or two edges that barely meet. To sew a hook and eye on overlapping edges, proceed as follows: Mark position for hook and eye. Using a double thread, sew hook in place ⅛ inch from edge on inside of overlap side, making sure stitches don't show on right side of fabric. Position and sew straight eye in place on outside of left side.

For edges that meet, proceed as follows: Sew hook on right inside of garment ⅛ inch from edge. (Have stitches go through eyelets but not to outer layer of fabric.) Stitch around eye, extending over edge on outside of opposite side.

Hooks and eyes.

Where stress on the closure is expected, hooks and eyes should be very serviceable. For lightweight fabrics and areas of little strain, substitute an eye of thread for the metal one.

Interfacing. Interfacing is a layer of fabric, applied to a facing or outer fabric. It is used for shaping, stabilization, and support. It can be woven, nonwoven, or fusible, and in most cases should not be heavier than the outer shell to which it is attached.

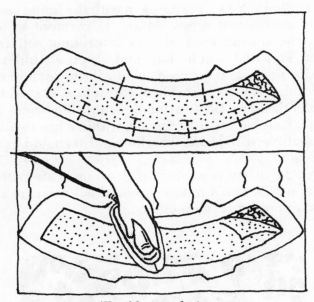

Fusible interfacing.

Interlining. Interlining is material used for added warmth. It is cut according to the lining pattern and can be constructed and

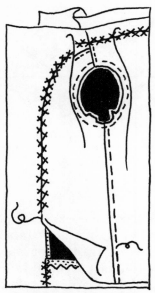

Interlining: Method 2.

attached to a garment by one of two methods. For the first of these proceed as follows: Sew interlining in with the lining seams. Trim seams, clip curves and press. Attach to garment as for normal lining. For the second method, sew interlining separately. Cut darts open, lap, and stitch. Lap and stitch shoulder and side seams. Trim seam allowance at neck. Trim remaining seams. Baste interlining loosely to inside of garment at seams, to within a few inches of the hem. Baste armhole seam allowances to those of outer fabric. Catchstitch to facings to within a few inches of hem. To be compatible with knits, interlining also should have stretch characteristics.

Jacquard. Jacquard is a fabric with an intricate pattern made by a special method on a unique apparatus known as a jacquard loom. It is a popular fashion choice.

Jacquard design.

Jersey. Jersey is a soft, plain, single-knit fabric used in clothing. A variation of tricot, it has excellent draping qualities and stretch characteristics.

Knit. A knit fabric is one made by intertwining yarn or thread, by machine or hand, in a series of connecting loops. (For types of knits, refer to the chapter on knit fabrics.)

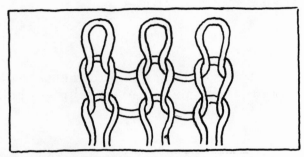

Intertwined yarn loops.

Knit stitch. The term knit stitch describes any of a variety of machine stitches characterized by give or elasticity. (Machine must be specially equipped.)

Knit stitches.

Layering. The process of grading or trimming seam allowances in an area of multiple thicknesses is called layering. The seam allowance closest to the outer fabric is the longest one.

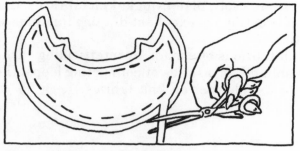
Layering.

Layout. Layout refers to the proper placement of pattern pieces on grain in woven fabrics and on a vertical rib in knit fabrics.

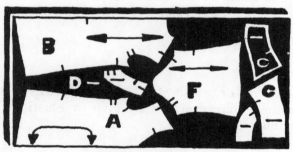
Pattern layout.

Marking. Marking refers to the transferring of pattern symbols such as darts, dots, buttonholes, and placement lines by visible means. (Several methods are described in the chapter on marking.)

Mitering. In sewing, mitering refers to a method of making trim, neat corners. To miter a band trim, proceed as follows: Position band along the finished edge of garment. Topstitch both band edges; stopping as indicated at lower edges. Fold remaining trim back on stitched trim, press the fold. Adjust and press trim, with a diagonal crease, along the edge to which it will be applied. Stitch the diagonal crease as indicated and topstitch along the remaining band edges.

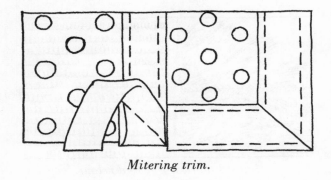

Mitering trim.

To miter pocket corners, proceed as follows: Press seam allowance to wrong side. Open out pressed seam allowance and fold diagonally through the point where the pressed seam allowance met. Press. Trim as indicated. Then fold seam allowance (with the diagonal crease) along the first lines pressed. Stitch.

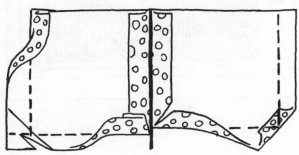

Mitering pocket.

Nap. Raised fibers from an underlying material such as velour and fur is called the nap. Examples of napped fabrics are stretch velours (velvet, velveteen, corduroy) and furs. The availability of this type of fabric affords variety in creative fashion.

When using a napped fabric, place all pattern pieces in the same direction to avoid characteristic shading of the fabric. When pressing, a piece of self fabric may be used as a press cloth. Steam is the secret ingredient — not pressure. Finish by gently brushing fabric in the direction of the pile.

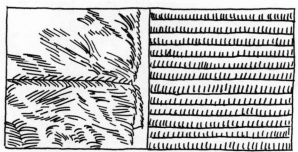

Napped fabrics: Fur and velour.

A needle board, which provides upright wires, can be used to prevent any matting of the nap. The right side of the fabric should be placed next to the wire network.

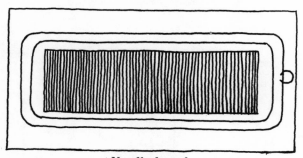

Needle board.

Neckline. The neckline is the upper edge of a garment which surrounds the neck or neck area. It can be finished in a variety of ways — with a collar (explained under C of this chapter) or facing (explained under F of this chapter).

A ribbed neckline, most often used on necklines without a closure, can be cut in any desired width to contrast or coordinate with fashion fabrics. Do not prewash as stretching might occur during the wash-and-dry process. For jewel, mock-turtle, and turtle necklines without closures, proceed as follows: Divide and mark neckline into four equal parts, using center front and back as first two markings. Ribbing length should equal two-thirds of neckline measurement plus seam allowance. The width equals twice the finished width plus one half inch seam allowance.

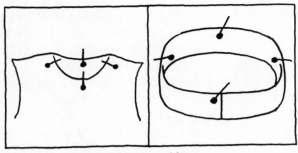

Ribbed neckline.

Before cutting ribbing, fit around head for comfortable fit. Divide and mark unstretched ribbing into four equal parts. Seam short ends and fold in half lengthwise, turning seam to the inside. Align right side of ribbing seam with right side of center back, raw edge to raw edge. Line up and pin remaining three markings. Using a stretch, zigzag, or straight stitch, and a ¼ inch seam allowance, stretch ribbing (which is on top) onto the neckline within each marked area. Press seam allowance toward body of the garment.

For a ruffled neckline proceed as follows: Cut, seam, and fold ribbing as above. Using a small zigzag stitch on the folded edge, stretch ribbing as you stitch zigzag half on and half off ribbing. A contrasting thread adds additional interest. Position trim to neckline, stitch, and press as above.

A self-fabric band neckline is usually used on necklines with closures. Proceed as follows: With the fabric stretch (crosswise rib), cut self-fabric the length of neckline measurement and twice the desired width, plus seam allowances. Fold lengthwise, right sides together, and stitch end seam allowance. Trim, turn, and press. Divide and mark neckline into fourths, starting with neckline opening. Divide and mark self-trim into fourths. With right

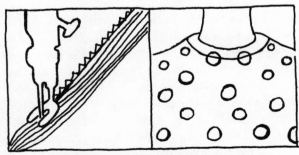

Ruffled (left) and self (right) necklines.

sides together, starting at opening, position and pin self-trim to garment at indicated markings. Stitch and press down seam allowance. A hook and eye may be necessary at opening, depending on width of trim.

To make a V-shaped neckline with self-trim, there are two methods which can be used. For method 1 proceed as follows: Decide finished width of trim you want, then double it and add ½ inch for seam allowance. Length will be measurement of the V plus one inch. Cut along the crosswise rib. Fold trim lengthwise. With right sides together, starting ⅛ inch from center of the V, pin and stitch trim with a ¼ inch seam allowance. Stretch trim only across back neckline. Stitch to within one or 1½ inches of center, depending on width of trim. Snip center of the V to the first stitch. Now turn trim right side up, with unstitched trim tucked behind the first stitched. Finish stitching on wrong side. Cut off excess trim. Press seam allowance down toward body of the garment. Transparent tape should be used to stabilize the center of the V below the stitching line before applying trim.

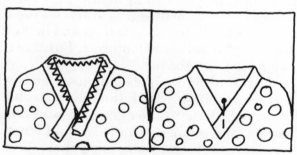

V-necklines with self-trim: Method 1.

For method 2 proceed as follows: Fold neck band lengthwise along foldline, wrong sides together. Baste raw edges together. On women's apparel lap right end of neck band over left end, matching pattern symbols. Baste together at seamline. Clip neck edge to the reinforced point of the V. With right sides together, pin neck band to neck edge matching center front and shoulder symbols. With a small zigzag, knit, or straight stitch, stitch neck band to neck edge, stretching if necessary. For a sharply pointed V, pivot (turn fabric with needle down, presser foot up) at center front when stitching. Grade seam. Press toward body of garment.

Other neckline finishes are described in detail elsewhere in this book.

V-neckline: Method 2.

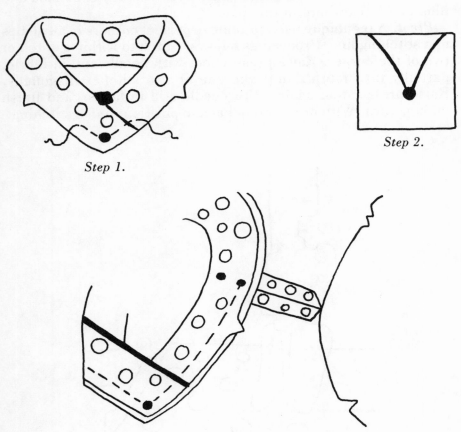

Step 1.

Step 2.

Step 3.

One-way design. This term refers to fabric with a design running in only one direction. Study fabric carefully for best effect and position all pattern pieces in only one direction, being certain to maintain the continuity of the design.

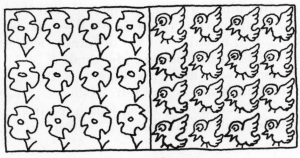

One-way designs.

Pants. Instruction for pants construction is fully explained and illustrated elsewhere in this book.

Pivot. A tecnhique used to achieve perfect corners in all angles of a stitching line. Proceed as follows: Stitch to within a stitch or two of the corner. Raise presser foot with needle still in fabric, partially turn fabric, and take one or two stitches diagonally. Raise presser foot again, with needle still in fabric, and finish making turn. With presser foot back in position, finish stitching.

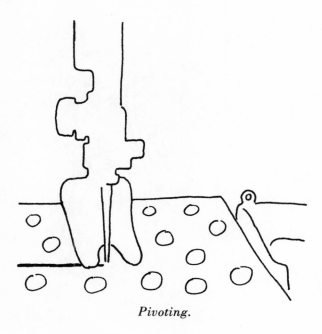

Pivoting.

Plaid. A plaid must first be distinguished as either even or uneven. If a plaid is even, it will be exactly the same to the right and left, and top and bottom, of the main bar—that is, the most predominant one. A fabric can have an uneven lengthwise plaid only, meaning that the design to the right and left of the main bar is different, while above and below the main bar it is the same. A fabric can have an uneven crosswise plaid — that is, the designs above and below the main bar are different, while the designs right and left of the main bar are identical. A plaid can also be uneven both lengthwise and crosswise.

Study a plaid carefully before purchasing it. An even plaid is easier to match than an uneven one, which requires careful planning. For matching plaids purchase ¼ to 1 yard extra, depending

76

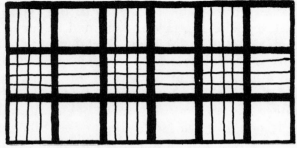

Even plaid.

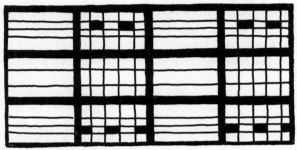

Uneven plaid.

on the size of the plaid. Select a pattern with few pattern pieces. Those patterns which are displayed in plaid are excellent choices. Most garments are matched horizontally, from the bottom up, because waist and bust darts will distort the matching. Notches of the same number will be seamed together, so position them exactly on the same bar. Usually, set-in sleeves cannot be matched at both the front and back armholes; therefore, choose a front match. The notch on the front of the sleeve will be positioned on the same bar as the notch on the front of the armhole. Even plaids can be cut doubly with an everage degree of success if bars are matched and pinned along the edges and at random throughout the fabric.

Match raglan sleeves at the front shoulder notches. Center back of collars should correspond with center back of garment. In matching a pocket to a garment, match both vertically and horizontally. To avoid matching, cut pocket on the diagonal; the contrast will be quite pleasing.

An uneven plaid should be cut on a single layer of fabric. Reverse the pattern piece for the second cutting, while still matching the bars. An easy way to match an uneven plaid is to use the cut piece in a reversed position.

Pocket. Pocket construction varies with the type pocket desired. For a patch pocket, square and unlined, proceed as follows: Turn top edge of pocket to the right side along foldline, forming the pocket facing. Stitch from top edge of one side completely around to the other. Pivot at corners. Trim upper corners and seams of pocket facing. Turn and press, folding back remaining seam allowance. Be sure corners have been mitered. Position pocket on right side of fabric, following pocket placement markings. Topstitch by machine or slipstitch by hand.

For an unlined patch pocket with rounded lower corners, proceed as follows: Progress as for unlined square pocket to completion of stitching line. Trim upper corners and seam allowance. At lower rounded corners, clip in notches to the stitching line along entire curve. Turn and press seam allowance with stitching underneath. Topstitch, edgestitch, or slipstitch in place on right side of garment.

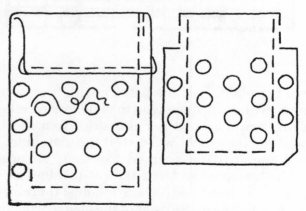

Patch pocket: Steps 1 and 2.

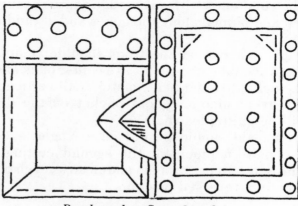

Patch pocket: Steps 3 and 4.

For a lined patch pocket proceed as follows: Cut lining according to the pocket pattern, but only to the foldline. Press under ⅝ inch on upper edge of lining and pin right side to right side of pocket. Turn facing to right side along foldline. Stitch from one upper edge, pivoting at corners, to other upper edge. Trim seam allowance and corners. Turn and press. Slipstitch lining to facing. Attach pocket as previously described.

Lined pocket.

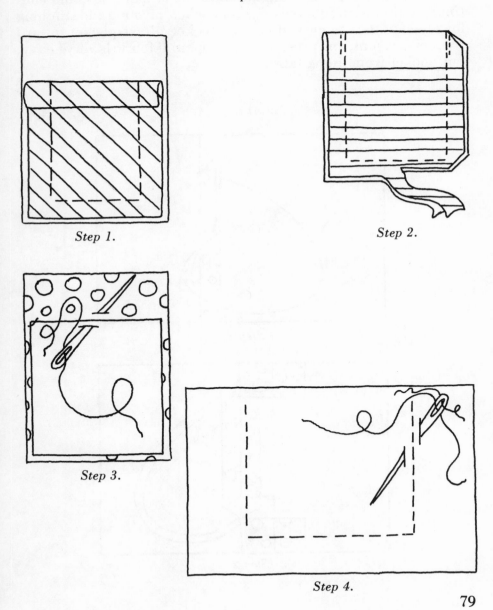

Step 1.

Step 2.

Step 3.

Step 4.

To stitch a pocket invisibly, baste it in place, keeping a straight stitching line. On the wrong side of the garment, handstitch in place, using the basting as a guide, and stitch only through lining and seam allowance.

For an inseam pocket proceed as follows: Match markings, and with right sides together, pin and stitch pocket pieces separately to extensions of garment made by clipping seam allowance to markings. Grade seams and press open. With right sides together, pin garment sections together, being careful to match markings. Stitch along seamline, pivoting at markings, and continue to stitch along curved edges of pocket, pivoting and stitching lower seam. Grade curved area of pocket. Press pocket toward front of garment, and press all seams open. If fabric is very heavy, cut pocket from lining fabric.

Pocket in seam.

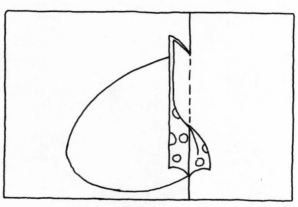

Step 1.

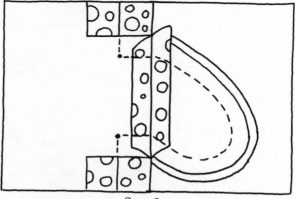

Step 2.

80

Pressing. A method of shaping utilizing heat and steam is called pressing. (For complete details refer to chapter on pressing.)

Quilting stitch. A quilting stitch is a running stitch that holds two layers of fabric together, adding more body. Quilting stitches are commonly used on under collars and lower lapels having woven or non-woven interfacing. However, if fusible interfacing is used, quilting stitches are not necessary.

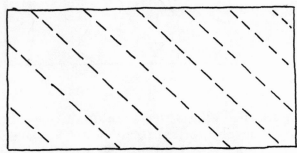

Quilting stitches.

Regulation stitch. A regulation stitch is the permanent straight stitch used to join two or more pieces of fabric together. For average-weight fabric, twelve to fifteen stitches per inch is normal. For fine fabric use shorter stitches; for heavier fabric use longer stitches.

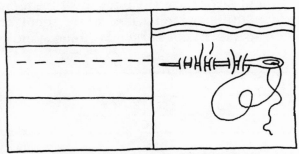

Stitches; Regulation and running.

Roll line. The roll line, identified as such on pattern, is the exact line on which a lapel is folded or rolled to the front of the garment. The quilting stitch, often referred to as the padding stitch, is done just inside the roll line and stops at the seamline.

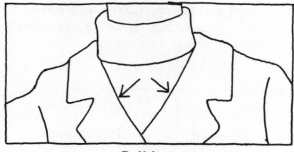

Roll line.

Running stitch. Running stitches are small, even hand stitches.

Satin stitch. Closely worked parallel stitches over small running stitches produce a satin stitch. Slant stitches for a straight line and conform to a curve by fanning stitches.

Seams. Seams are the very foundation of your fashion creation; construct them with perfection. Seams hold a garment together. They should be smooth, unstretched, and unpuckered. Seams are of numerous types, each type serving a different purpose and requiring a different procedure. Structural seams include the plain (straight) seam, the eased seam, the curved seam, and the corner seam. The decorative seams include the flat-felled seam, the lapped seam, the tucked seam, the welt seam, the corded seam, and the raised seam. All of these are discussed below.

Plain or straight seams are the ones most frequently encountered. They are often ⅝ inch wide, while some knit patterns require ¼-inch seams. Exact seam allowance is indicated on the

Seams: ⅝ inch and ¼ inch.

pattern and the instruction sheet. To construct a plain seam, proceed as follows: With right sides together, match and pin edges, top and bottom of seams, and notches. Always pin toward the middle. Pins should be through the seamline and perpendicular to the edge. (Most machines will stitch over pins placed in this manner.) Knit fabrics may require more pins to help control stretching. Stitch on stitching line, using directional stitching and 12 to 15 stitches per inch. Press seam.

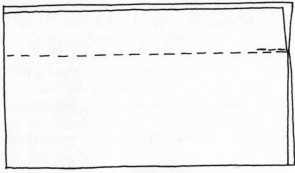

Plain seam.

An eased seam is used to join a larger section to a smaller one. To work an eased seam on stable knit, proceed as follows: On the larger section, stitch a gathering stitch between notches, approximately ½ inch from the seam edge. With the larger side on top, match markings and pin sections together. Draw ease thread until the larger section fits the smaller section. Knot ends of thread and distribute fullness evenly. Pin and stitch. To shrink out fullness, press the two layers together, with the eased section on top. Press seam open. When you encounter only slight fullness, roll fabric over index finger and use thumbs to ease it in. Use many pins to avoid puckers. Stitch carefully, adjusting fabric if necessary to avoid puckering.

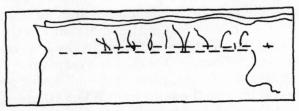

Eased seam.

To work an eased seam on stretch knit, follow directions for plain seam. The smaller pattern piece goes on top. In the area to be eased, stretch smaller piece to coincide with the larger one as you stitch. With this technique, it is best not to pin the eased area.

Curved seams are constructed like plain seams, but require more detailing. To work a curved seam, proceed as follows: With right sides together, pin the two like curved edges together, matching notches and markings. Stitch. The curve may be either an outward curve, such as on a collar or pocket, or an inward curve such as the underarm seam of a sleeve. An outward seam should be notched by cutting small, triangular sections from the seam allowance at evenly spaced intervals. To determine the width and number of notches to be cut, turn the seam to the position it will take on the finished garment. The excess material will form ripples similar to ruffles. Crease the ripple and cut the excess away. If properly trimmed, the pressed-out seam will have no further ripples. An inward curve should be clipped or snipped at regular intervals, depending on the depth of the curve. A sufficiently clipped seam, when pressed, is smooth and shows no sign of strain.

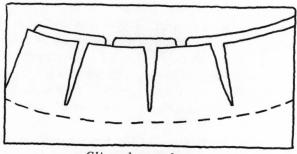

Clipped curved seam.

Perfect corner seams can be attained by following a few simple rules. With right sides together, match notches and markings, pinning toward the center. Stitch along stitching line directly to the corner. Raise presser foot with needle still in the garment. Turn corner slightly. With presser foot in the lowered position, take one or two stitches across the corner. Again raise presser foot with needle still in the fabric, pivot material, lower presser foot, and continue stitching on the same line. When stitching an inward corner follow the same procedure, but reinforce the inward corner

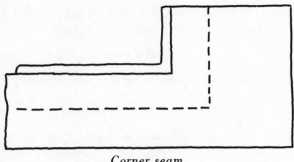

Corner seam.

one inch before and after the point. This may be done using small stitches just inside the seamline or by stitching a one-inch square of fabric on the seamline for extra strength. Clip to point. Trim and press seam.

So far, structural seams have been described. Now some decorative seams that are quite often used with knits will be introduced.

A flat-felled seam is made by placing wrong sides together, and matching notches and top and bottom of seam. Pin toward the middle and stitch on stitching line. Press both seam allowances in the same direction. Trim underlying seam to ⅛ inch. Turn in raw edge of upper seam allowance ¼ inch. Topstitch or edgestitch to garment encasing underlying seam.

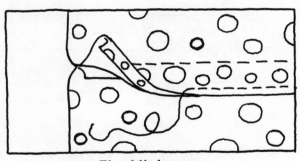

Flat-felled seam.

A lapped seam is constructed by pressing the ⅝ inch seam allowance on one section to the wrong side. It is then placed on the other section, seamlines matching and pinned. Raw edges will now be even on the underneath side. On the right side of the fabric, edgestitch or topstitch along the seamline. Grade and press seam allowances in the same direction.

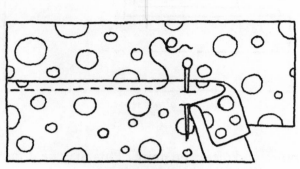

Lapped seam.

A tucked seam is made in much the same manner, with the following exception. Instead of stitching on the stitching line, the desired depth of the tuck will determine the seamline. A row of regulation stitches or topstitching can then be used.

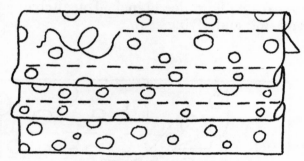

Tucked seam.

A welt seam is the reverse of a flat-felled seam. It is constructed with right sides together, by stitching on the seamline. Press both seam allowances to one side, and trim the underseam allowance to ⅛ inch. On outside of garment, stitch through fabric and untrimmed seam allowance, encasing the trimmed seam allowance.

The last three seam finishes just mentioned help to eliminate that 'unpressed seam' look often encountered with knits.

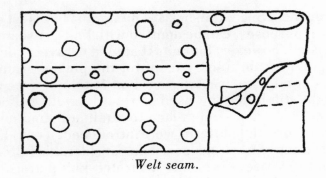

Welt seam.

A corded seam is made by first encasing cording within a bias strip. Using a cording or zipper foot, stitch close to cording. Pin encased cording, with raw edges together, to upper section of fabric. Pin and stitch. Pin this section of fabric to the remaining section, right sides together. With corded layer on top, machine stitch on wrong side close to visible line of stitching. Grade seams and press.

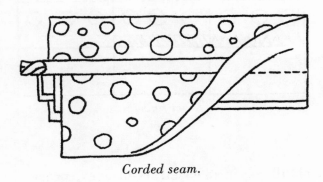

Corded seam.

A raised seam is often desirable along the crease line of women's and children's pants. In other areas it is often used to give a decorative effect. A raised seam in pants can be accomplished in two ways:

1. Press the crease in the pants front. Fold along crease line and machine edgestitch with the grain.

2. A special foot is usually attached for the double-needle method. A raised seam is then sewn with tightened tension, while the front pant sections remain free. Press crease in desired position. On right side, stitch directionally along the crease with the section flat not folded.

Seam finishes. Seam finishes are numerous but most often, for all practical purposes, can be omitted with knits. A seam finish is recommended, however, for knits that tend to ravel. You may use any acceptable seam finish except for the pinked seam and the turned-under edge seam. A zigzag, knit stitch, or even a regulation straight stitch may be used to retard raveling. For a more decorative finish, use stretch lace to attain a bound edge.

Sleeves. Before knit patterns were introduced, it could be safely said that the cap of a set-in sleeve had considerable fullness. This is no longer the case, especially in stretch-knit patterns. Proper construction for an eased set-in sleeve will be discussed first, followed by sewing directions for raglan and kimono sleeves.

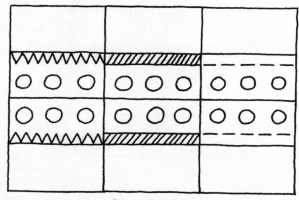

Seam finishes.

To control fullness in an eased set-in sleeve proceed as follows: Stitch a row of gathering stitches just inside the stitching line, from one notch to the other. With right sides together and notches matching, pin and stitch sleeve seam. With right sides together, pin set-in sleeve to garment with notches, symbols, and seams matching. Pull the ease stitching or gathering stitches until sleeve cap fits within the notched area. Distribute fullness evenly. Pin closely, easing out fullness with your thumbs as you progress around the armhole. Starting at either the front or the back notch, stitch around the sleeve carefully, easing in fullness, and ending stitching line at the opposite notch. By proceeding in this manner, the under sleeve, most susceptible to strain, will have a double row of stitches. Clip and trim underarm seam to approximately ¼ inch. Grade remaining seam allowance and clip where necessary.

Eased set-in sleeve.

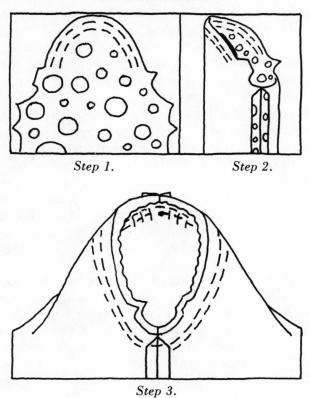

Step 1. Step 2.

Step 3.

Using a pressing ham, shrink out fullness in the sleeve cap by pressing both the sleeve and armhole seams together from the sleeve side. Use tip of iron only and press along stitching line. Further fullness can be reduced by pressing the sleeve cap on the wrong side and from the sleeve side to the stitching line, easing out fullness as you press. A small traveling iron is most beneficial for pressing sleeves.

When using a pattern for knits only, you may encounter a sleeve that is just an inch or so larger than the armhole. If so, proceed as follows: With right sides together, stitch and press open the sleeve seam. With right sides together and notches matching, position the sleeve in the armhole. The sleeve cap will be easier to apply if you pin only at the notches and the shoulder seam. Then, with the sleeve on bottom and the armhole on top, proceed to stitch from one notch, continuing around the sleeve to the other notch. As you approach the smaller section, stretch the material while you stitch until the smaller area fits the larger one. Progressing in this manner, double stitch the underarm or stress area. If a ⅝-inch seam allowance has been used, trim underarm seam at notches to approximately ¼ inch. Clip seam. Trim and grade upper portion of sleeve, and press as previously described. If you used a ¼-inch seam allowance while constructing the seam (as is often the case with knit patterns), there will be no seam allowance to grade or trim. Clip underarm portion of seam if necessary.

When constructing this type of sleeve, you may also employ the open-seam method. With right sides together, match notches, symbols, and pin. With sleeve on bottom and armhole on top, stitch from one edge to the other, stretching and stitching upper section to correspond with the bottom section. In one continuous operation, stitch sleeve seam and side garment seam. Press sleeve seam and side-garment seam. If you used a ⅝-inch seam allowance, trim and clip underarm and cap seam as previously described. If you have used a ¼-inch seam allowance, clip where necessary.

A raglan sleeve is constructed easily by the open-seam method. Proceed as follows: First, stitch darts in shoulder portion of sleeve and press darts open. Stitch elbow darts where indicated and press downward. With right sides together, matching notches and symbols, pin sleeve to garment front and back. Stitch seams, clip curves, and press open. Join underarm seam of sleeve and garment side seam in one continuous operation. Clip seam where necessary and press.

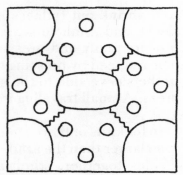

Raglan sleeve: Open seam.

A raglan sleeve can also be set in. In this method the garment side seam, shoulder dart, and sleeve seam are stitched before remaining sleeve and garment seams are matched and stitched. Seam allowances are then clipped and pressed open.

Raglan sleeve: Closed seam.

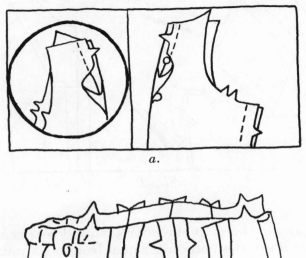

a.

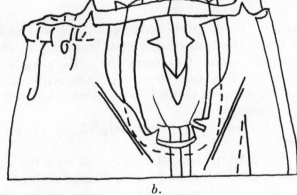

b.

For a kimono sleeve proceed as follows: With right sides together, notches and markings matching, pin and stitch garment

Kimono sleeve.

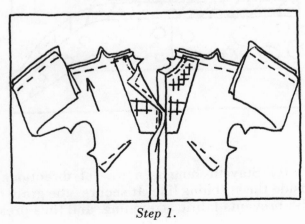

Step 1.

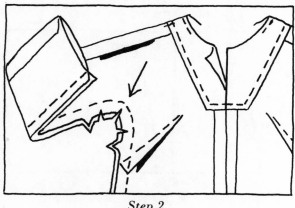

Step 2.

front and garment back at shoulder seams. Press seams. With right sides still together, stitch garment front to garment back at underarm and side seams. Reinforce the underseam with a piece of woven seam binding one to two inches wide, stitching on stitching line. Clip curve of underarm seam, but not the seam binding. Press seam open.

A sleeve board will prove very helpful for pressing all the sleeves described above.

Slipstitch. A slipstitch is one that is invisible on the right side of a garment, and is generally used for hems and facings. It is made by picking up one or two threads of the fabric and loosely catching the needle in the hem edge.

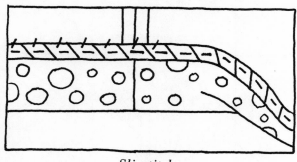

Slipstitch.

Staystitching. Staystitching is a row of directional stitches sewn just inside the stitching line. It secures the grain threads or ribs properly, prevents fabric stretching, and thus preserves the pattern line. Most patterns indicate the proper direction for stitching.

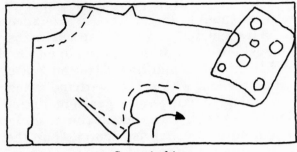

Staystitching.

Stay. A stay is used to keep a seam from stretching. It can be of woven fabric or of bias tape or even thread. For a tape stay, proceed as follows: Cut the tape the length of the area to which it will be applied. Pin the tape to the stitching line, with approximately ¼ inch extending toward the garment. Stitch, grade, and press seam open.

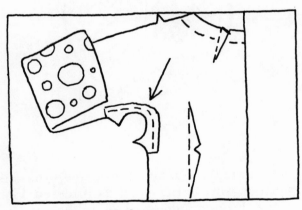

Underarm stay.

A double strand of thread makes a lightweight stay that will not inhibit the flexibility of a knit. Proceed as follows: Cut the thread double the length of the area to which it will be applied. Place the thread on the seam stitching line. With a small zigzag or knit stitch, stitch over the thread as you progress over the stitching line. Trim seam and press.

Snap. Snaps are garment fasteners, and are available in many varieties and sizes. They are clear, silver-toned, or black, and range in size from small to large. Choose size according to the fabric weight and expected strain. To attach snaps proceed as follows: Mark position of snaps in usual manner. On the overlapping side, anchor thread on marking. Place snap with protrusion over thread and proceed, with small overhand stitches, to stitch through one opening, picking up a garment thread with each stitch. Continue stitching by carrying the thread under the snap to the next opening until the snap is secured. Lap the sewn snap section over the remaining garment section at the point to which the socket section will be sewn. Press firmly. Anchor thread in the depression left by the upper snap. Place socket in position, and secure as other snap section.

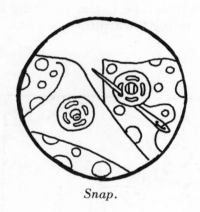

Snap.

Extended snaps are used to fasten two edges that just meet. To achieve this effect, sew upper snap as directed. Secure under snap by stitching through only one hole to the garment, with the remainder of the snap extending beyond the garment edge.

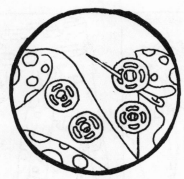

Extended snaps.

Texture. Texture refers to the appearance of a fabric, reflecting the arrangement of its yarns or fibers. Its surface may be flat and smooth, rough, or dimensional.

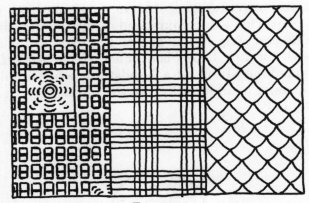

Textures.

Tailoring. The term tailoring refers to the art of perfectly fitting and constructing a garment. Tailoring will be further explained and illustrated later on in this book.

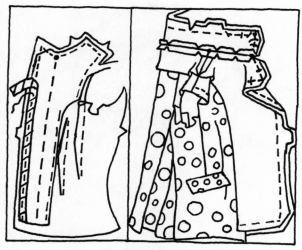

Tailoring.

Tape fastener. A tape fastener is a quick, easy closure used in place of more conventional fasteners. It is made of nylon and consists of two strips—one composed of tiny points, the other of loops. The looped strip is stitched to the overlap for flexibility. The tape with the tiny hooks is stitched to the underlap. Use a regulation machine stitch or a handstitch when applying both strips. If you use a machine stitch on the top layer, stitch the tape to the facing only.

Tape fastener.

Threader. A threader is a very simple gadget with a large eye that eliminates the eye-straining job of threading a needle. Insert the closed eye of the threader through the eye of the needle, then open the threader eye somewhat and thread it. Close the large eye and, together with the thread, pull it through the eye of the needle.

A needle threader accompanies most packages of hand needles.

Needle threader.

Trims. Working with trims can be a most enjoyable part of making and individualizing your clothes, so don't hesitate to have lots of fun with them. The many varied sizes, shapes, and forms, in which trimming can be found serve to enhance the beauty of a garment. Fabric trim should have the same characteristics as the garment fabric. When fabric is washed and dried prior to cutting, the trim should be treated in the same manner.

Strips of polyester trim come in varying widths, colors, and pattern combinations. They are applied on the right side of the garment, in the area desired, and can be stitched with a zigzag or regulation machine stitch.

Monograms, which personalize garments, can be applied by machine or hand. To monogram by hand, proceed as follows: First trace the design of the monogram lightly on the the right side of the garment. If the fabric to be worked is lightweight, a thin backing may be necessary. Place fabric in an embroidery hoop until taut. Secure knotted thread on the underside of the fabric. Satin stitch (a very close overhand stitch) around the entire monogram. Finish by again securing threads on the underside of the fabric. Trim backing close to stitches and press. (Pressing on the wrong side on a terry towel will not depress the stitches and will give more dimension to the monogram.)

To monogram by machine, proceed as follows: First trace the design on the right side of the fabric, then place fabric tautly in an embroidery hoop. Adjust your machine to zigzag stitch of desired width. Drop the feed and hand move the hoop as you stitch around the entire monogram. Secure threads on the underside and press. If backing has been applied, trim close to stitching.

Bangles and beads can be purchased as single units or pre-strung. Attach them to the garment by handstitching from the inside of the garment to the outside, and then backstitching through the garment. Any number of desirable effects can be obtained.

Monogram.

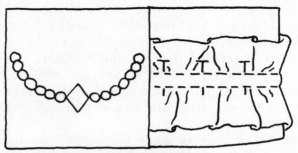

Trims: Prestrung beads (left) and ruffle (right).

Ruffles, used as frilly decorative trim can be any width; but the length of the ruffle should be at least two to three times the length of the area to be trimmed. Ruffles can be cut on the bias or the straight of grain. A ruffle can be a single ruffle with one free edge narrowly hemmed, or it can be a double ruffle with both edges folded in to where the gathering stitches will be placed. In either case, a gathering stitch is sewn along the raw edge of the single ruffle, or down the middle of the double ruffle, and pulled or gathered in the usual manner. It is then stitched to the garment with a regulation machine stitch along the gathering line.

Rickrack and braid trim are applied to the designated area of the garment by making a single row of zigzag or regulation stitches through the center of the trim. If they are applied before seams are sewn, their edges will be concealed on the underside of the garment. If applied after the garment is finished, it will be necessary to fold in an edge or edges so that no raw edge is visible when completed.

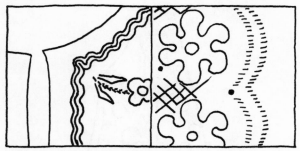

Trims: rickrack (left) and lace (right).

Lace, one of the oldest and most consistently popular of all trims, falls into two categories: (1) edging, which has one straight and one decorative edge, and (2) insertion, which has two identical edges. Attaching lace to a garment can be done painstakingly by hand or by machine. To trim an unfinished edge with lace, proceed as follows: Place the lace on the right side of the garment, raw edges together, and edgestitch. Turn lace downward and press. Another method is to turn under and press ¼ inch of the raw edge. Lap edge approximately ⅛ inch over lace, and edge-stitch.

If lace, either flat or gathered, is to be inserted within a seam, proceed as follows: First sew it to one section of the fabric along the seamline on the front of the fabric, with the lace extending into the main portion of that section. With right sides together, stitch remaining garment section to lace-trimmed section along stitching line. Press seam open, then press lace into desired position.

To use the insertion method, proceed as follows: Position lace over marked area. Pin and stitch along both edges. On back of garment, trim out material close to both edges of stitching. Raw edges may be finished with a small zigzag stitch and pressed away from the lace. Lace may be pieced by carefully matching design, and edgestitching with a fine zigzag. Trim close to seam.

Topstitching. Topstitching is a special effect often used by high-fashion designers. It is a decorative stitching done on the right side of the fabric. Usually the home sewer finds topstitching to be most conveniently done while the garment is being constructed. Proceed as follows: Mark area to be topstitched very accurately. (A seam guide, quilting foot, or tape made especially for this purpose can be used for perfect stitching.) Place two spools of thread on machine spindles, and thread the machine needle twice. You should now have two upper threads of the same consistency and one bobbin thread of a like consistency. Set

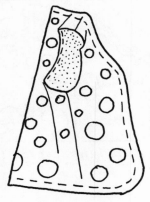

Topstitching.

stitch length at its longest position, and you are ready to sew. If you topstitch while constructing a garment, you need not worry about loose end threads. If topstitching is done after garment is completed, make sure the loose end threads are long enough to be threaded through to the wrong side and then securely knotted. For a more raised effect, stitch over tissue paper and tear away when finished.

Tuck. A tuck is a tiny pleat which is stitched along its entire length by hand or by machine. Tucks can be evenly or unevenly spaced. To produce tucks, proceed as follows: On the right side of the garment, mark the position and depth of tucks, and space from fold to fold. Stitch tuck from right side of fabric with a regulation machine stitch. When tucking is completed, press underside of each tuck. Turn to the wrong side and press the entire tucked area with a pressing cloth or a double layer of nylon netting. Brown paper strips placed between each tuck will eliminate image show-through.

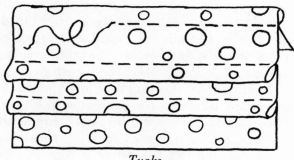

Tucks.

100

Understitching. Understitching is used to prevent a facing from peeking out to the right side of a garment. It is accomplished as follows: Fold both the seam allowance and the facing away from the body of a garment. Machine stitch together very close to the entire length of the seamline. Grade seams, clip where necessary, and turn to the inside of the garment. When pressing, slightly roll the seamline to the inside of the garment.

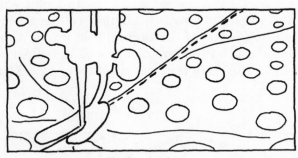

Understitching.

Vent. Vents are openings commonly found in the back or sides of men's, women's, and children's clothing. When constructing a center vent, proceed as follows: Fold, stitch, and press seam allowance to wrong sides on both underlap and overlap sections. Stitch center back seam one-half inch past vent opening and press. Position overlap section along facing foldline and press. On top underlap, make a diagonal clip to the stitching line. Position underlap as indicated and pin. On outside of garment topstitch back seam, pivoting one-half inch past vent opening and stitching across it. Press. When hemming garment, make the underlap slightly shorter than the overlap section.

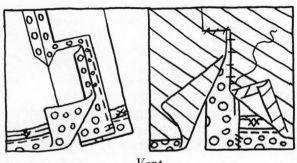

Vent.

Waistband. A waistband is a finishing technique used on skirts and pants. Several types of waistbands are described below. A self-waistband is one which is made with a facing to give the appearance of no waistband at all. The facing may be of self-fabric, fabric of lighter weight, or ribbon. To construct a self-waistband proceed as follows: With right sides together, matching notches and symbols, pin and stitch facing to waistband. (To maintain shape and eliminate stretching, a length of grosgrain ribbon extending ⅛ inch over the seamline may be stitched at the same time.) Understitch facing, grade seam, clip where necessary. Turn and press downward, slightly rolling the seamline to the inside. On both ends of the facing, fold under approximately ⅝ inch and handstitch facing to ribbon of zipper. A hook and eye may be added to the underside of the facing for extra security.

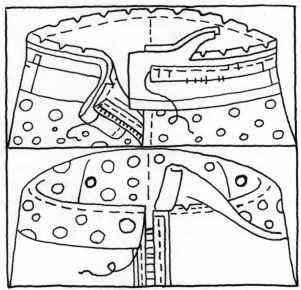

Self-waistband with fabric facing.

When using grosgrain ribbon as facing, choose a width approximately ¾ inch to one inch wide. Be certain to preshrink and press it before use. When pressing, shape one edge of ribbon so that it is longer than the other, to correspond to a waistline edge. The length of the ribbon should equal the waistline measurement plus approximately 1¼ inches, and should be measured on the shorter edge of the ribbon. Proceed as follows: Staystitch along the waist-line just inside seam allowance and trim to ¼ inch. Clip where necessary. Lap and pin ribbon over the line of staystitches, with ⅝ inch extending beyond both edges. Edgestitch, turn, and press, slightly rolling the seamline to the inside. Turn under the ⅝-inch extensions on both sides and handstitch to the zipper ribbon.

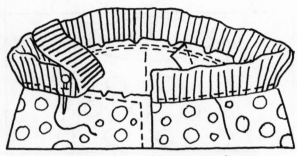

Self-waistband with grosgrain facing.

When constructing a rolled elastic waistband, use appropriate elastic approximately ¾ inch wide. The length of the elastic should equal the waist measurement less one-two inches. Proceed as follows: Narrow-seam raw edges together. Mark and divide into four equal parts. Divide partially constructed waistline into four equal parts and mark. Pin elastic to the wrong side of waistline at markings. With waistline on bottom and elastic on top, proceed to stitch lower edge of elastic in place with a small to medium zigzag stitch, stretching elastic to fit between markings. When done, turn the waistline to the inside, the width of the elastic. With a zigzag stitch, stitch through all thickness on the lower edge of turned waistline. Press. This type of waistband is usually not used on a garment with a waist closure.

A conventional waistband can be sewn in three easy steps. Proceed as follows: First, fold waistband lengthwise and stitch ends from fold to within ⅝ inch of the edge. A fusible interfacing can be pressed to the notched side within the seam allowances. Grade seam and turn. Press seams and turn under ⅝ inch on the unnotched side. With right sides together and notches matching, pin waistband to waistline edge. Stitch. Press seam allowance up, grade, and clip where necessary. Pin pressed area to inside of skirt just below the stitching line. On right side of garment, stitch in the ditch (seam depression) which will attach the under portion

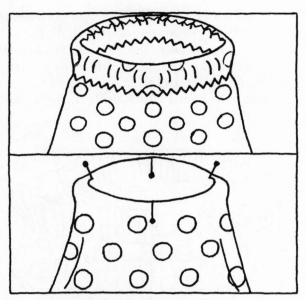

Rolled elastic waistband.

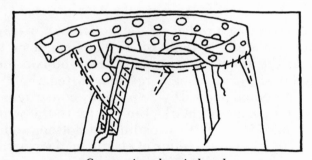

Conventional waistband.

of the waistband. If the under portion of the waistband is to be stitched by hand, position and pin it slightly above the stitching line. Handstitch and press well.

A waistband cut onto a garment is constructed and pressed as one with the upper section of the skirt or pants. Proceed as follows: On the uppermost section of the garment, stitch along edge with a knit, zigzag, or straight stitch. Cut a ribbon stay 1¼ inch longer than the waist measurement. Place on foldline with ends of stay even with edges of garment. Edgestitch along foldline. Turn facing to inside of garment along foldline and press. Complete closure as for a fabric facing after inserting zipper.

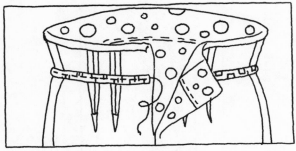

Cut-on waistband.

Welt. A welt is detailed under "Pockets" in this section.

Yarn. A continuous strand of twisted thread used in woven or knitted fabrics. It can be made of cotton, wool, flax, or a snythetic such as polyester and nylon, or a combination of any of these materials. The yarn composition of a fabric influences its characteristics.

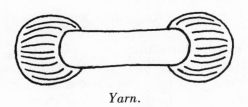

Yarn.

Zipper adhesive. Zipper adhesive is a narrow, double-faced tape. Place it at the outer edge, on the right side of the zipper tape, for ease in inserting. With contrasting thread, baste zipper opening on the garment closed, and press seam open. Remove upper layer from zipper adhesive and, with tab up, place face down and centered over the basted seam. Using a zipper foot, stitch zipper to garment. Release basting thread and press.

Zipper. Zippers are manufactured in standard lengths and popular colors. There are conventional zippers appropriate for most garments, and special purpose for jackets and pants. There are zippers with exposed metal coils attached to cotton tape, covered nylon zippers attached to nylon tape, and featherweight polyester zippers attached to mesh-like polyester. After prewashing and drying, these zippers are all inserted in a similar manner.

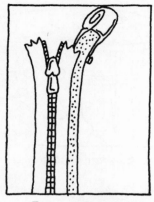

Zipper adhesive.

(The invisible zipper, discussed later, which is hidden within a seam, requires special application.) The following is standard procedure for all conventional zippers:

1. Press zipper tape only, with coils facing downward. Pressing on a terry towel is ideal.
2. Use a zipper or cording foot.
3. Be sure the coils of the zipper are below the ⅝-inch seam allowance.
4. Zippers can be positioned with pins, tape, or basting.

For center or slot application, baste the zipper seam closed with contrasting thread, and press seam open. Position zipper face down and centered over basted seam, with tab up. Secure position prior to stitching. From the inside of the garment, stitch down one side, across lower end of zipper, and upward along raised stitching line on zipper tape. If zipper tape does not have an indicated stitching line, then zipper foot should glide against the coils as you stitch.

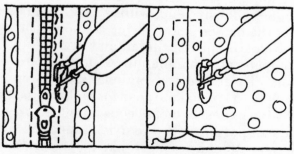

Slot Zipper applications.

A standard zipper may also be stitched from the right side of the garment in a similar manner. Stitching line should then be approximately ¼ inch from the placket fold. Remove basting and complete facing as directed. Be certain that facing ends, when stitched, do not obstruct the zipper.

A lapped zipper requires a somewhat different procedure. Most zipper manufacturers include illustrated instructions for a lapped zipper application. A quick and easy lapped application is described here. Proceed as follows: Turn back and press the ⅝-inch seam allowance on the zipper opening on both sides. On the right side, properly position and secure the closed zipper to the left opening section. Fabric should be very close to coils, but not obstructing them. Stitch directionally. Position and secure overlap edge to zipper tape, hiding first line of stitching. Stitch across lower end of zipper, from seamline and upward, approximately ½ inch from edge of the fabric. Finish facing as previously described.

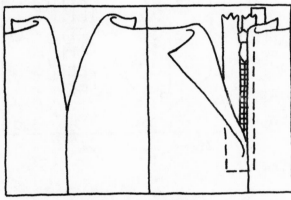

Easy lapped zipper.

A decorative zipper is a regular zipper with braid or trim added for a decorative effect. This zipper is positioned and stitched from the outside of the garment.

So far, installation of zippers within seams has been described. The following describes a zipper application without a seam: First, cut a stay from lightweight fabric or interfacing, the length of the zipper plus one inch, and double the entire width of the zipper. Center and secure this on the outside of the garment section in which the zipper will appear. Mark center line. Draw a box around the center line, the width and length of the zipper coils. Stitch on this line. Cut along center line and to each corner. Turn stay to the inside and press firmly along stitching line. Position zipper tape with coils exposed within this opening. The end of the zipper coils will be even with the lower edge of the box. The other two edges of the fabric will be positioned and secured close to the edge of the coils, but not obstructing them. Edgestitch along lower end of opening and upward; stitch in like manner on other edge. (This zipper may also be applied from the inside by stitching along seam allowance of wedge, fabric, and tape.) Secure the lower end by stitching across the stay and the lower end of the zipper tape. For both methods, press.

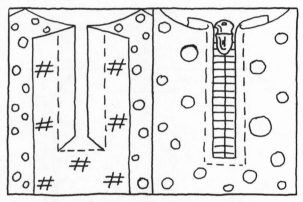

Zipper without a seam.

An invisible zipper is a hidden zipper sewn within a seam. It requires a special application and a special zipper foot which can be purchased with the zipper. Proceed as follows: Open zipper and place it face down in a terry cloth. Press coils open. Leave seam to which it will be applied entirely open and unpressed. Place the right side of the zipper against the right side of the fabric, with raw edges together. Stitching from the top of the zipper, position the zipper foot so that the ridged area will ride on the coils. Stitch down to zipper pull and secure. To position remaining side, close zipper. The right side of the zipper tape will again face the right side of the fabric, with raw edges together. Open zipper and position ridged area of zipper foot over the coils.

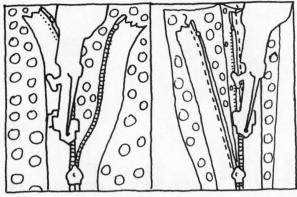

Invisible zipper.

Stitch from top to zipper pull. Secure. Remove invisible zipper foot and attach a zipper or standard hinged foot. Stitch entire length of seam closed, including the portion left unstitched at the lower end of the zipper. Be careful to end on the original stitching line. Stitch lower edges of the zipper tape to the seam allowance for approximately one inch, then finish garment in usual manner.

9

Just Between the Two of Us –
Hints Worth Knowing

— Knits are easy to sew.
— Use ballpoint pins or weights for placement.
— A new ballpoint needle for every garment will eliminate snags and pulls.
— A small-holed throat plate will lessen knotting of thread to fabric.
— Stitching is easier with a hinged or roller presser foot.
— Start stitching with long threads pulled to the rear of the presser foot until stitching is past the raw edge of the material.
— To avoid snags when inserting fabric under the presser foot, lower the feed dogs. Raise to begin stitching.
— A zigzag is a less sophisticated stretch stitch.
— A small zigzag stitch can be used even in structural seams.
— Stitching directionally (with the vertical rib) helps to insure a good fit.
— Little soap pieces make good markers; the marks are easy to remove.
— Use twelve to fifteen stitches per inch for most knits.
— On most knits, seams do not have to be clean finished.
— Do not let fabric drag as you sew. It stretches.
— A double layer of nylon net makes an excellent pressing cloth—it lets steam penetrate, keeps off shine. Use wool or synthetic setting on iron.

- A needle threader inserted from the wrong to the right side, and then to a pulled yarn, will take the misguided yarn back out of sight.
- Paper inserted beneath seams will eliminate image show-through to the right side.
- Vertical buttonholes stretch less than horizontal ones.
- To control buttonhole stretch, work buttonhole over heavy thread or cord.
- Plaids less than ¼" need not be matched.
- When clipping, use only the point of the scissors, and never clip past the stitching line.
- When cutting dark-colored velvet, cut with nap running up for a richer color.
- When cutting light-colored velvet, cut with nap running down for a frosted look.
- Cut notches out, not off.
- Two rows of stitches will keep the hem of a heavy knit from sagging. Stitch first row with the hem folded in half, second row in the usual place.
- Never cut paper heavier than tissue with fabric shears—it dulls them.
- A pattern should never be cut out with pinking shears.
- To shorten a zipper, stitch a thread stop where you want the zipper to end. Allow room for stitching, then cut off.
- Thread a shade darker than the fabric will sew a shade lighter.
- Seams will be pucker-free if you hold the fabric under slight tension as you sew.
- Use compatible needle and thread to avoid skipped stitches.
- Maintain a smooth rhythm when stitching.
- Use a loose thread and a properly balanced stitch.
- Needle and thread sizes should be related.
- To make zipper application quicker and easier, use zipper adhesive—it avoids pinning or basting.
- When basting on light-colored fabrics, use a contrasting, but not dark, thread.
- Test thread tension by stitching a double thickness of the fabric to be sewn.
- To avoid sit out or flattened nap, cut velvet with the nap running up.
- When matching an uneven plaid, cut singly. Use the cut piece reversed for a perfect match.
- Before pressing a seam open, first press flat as it was sewn. This helps to straighten out the seam line.

- It is best to hang a stable-knit garment overnight before hemming.
- Use stitching tape for a perfect topstitching guide.
- A double strand of thread makes prominent topstitching.
- Do not use bias woven or designed fabric for bias-cut patterns.
- Zigzagging over a double strand of thread makes a serviceable, lightweight stay.
- Always cut panne velvet with the nap running down.
- To prolong the shape of an A-line hem, interface with bias strips.
- The lengthwise rib of a knit is considered the straight grain.
- Selvage need not be cut away, but should be clipped when sewn.
- For plaids, use a pattern with few seams.
- When using elastic thread for shirring, hand-wind it onto the bobbin. Mercerized thread works well on the top.
- Brush out your bobbin case often to prevent a build-up of lint which will affect stitching quality—also damages your machine.
- For a diagonal plaid, use a pattern with few seams.
- An electric scissors will make short work of cutting.
- No need to lock (back stitch) a seam if it will be crossed by another seam.
- A travel iron is a good accessory for pressing set-in sleeves.
- For easier threading, cut thread on the diagonal.
- Use a clean bobbin for each winding as threads of different consistencies cause uneven winding.
- A low speed or a low gear is best for heavy or bulky fabrics.

Part III

10
And Away We Sew

Familiar techniques should not be forgotten. However, in some instances they should be interpreted differently. In this chapter knit techniques and quick methods of garment construction, dis-

Knit fashions.

cussed in previous chapters, have been adapted to typical pattern situations for your convenience. If you apply them diligently to similar situations, you will have made a smooth transition from sewing with woven to knit fabrics.

You will confidently look forward to sewing a completely new wardrobe of fashion's finest fibers—and with the greatest of ease.

TOP WITH V-NECK AND WAIST RIB TRIM

1. Stay stitch front neck edge.
    a. Reinforce center-front neck edge with another row of stitches close to the first row.

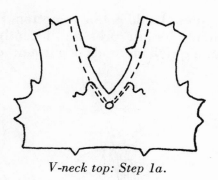

V-neck top: Step 1a.

    b. Staystitch back neck edge. Pin and stitch front to back at shoulder seams. Press seams.

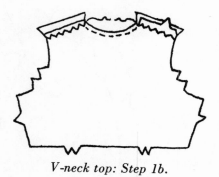

V-neck top: Step 1b.

2. Attach neck band to center-front neck edge. (Detailed directions are given for V-neck bands under "Neckline" in Part 2.)
3. Stitch back to front at side seams. Press.

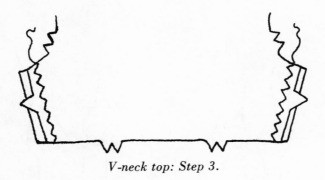

V-neck top: Step 3.

4. With right sides together, stitch waist ribbing, forming a tube. Turn right side out. Fold in half along foldline. Divide and mark into four equal sections.

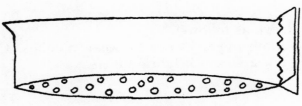

V-neck top: Step 4.

5. To attach ribbing to waist, proceed as follows.
    a. Divide and mark waist area of top into four equal sections.

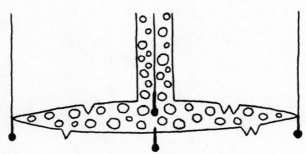

V-neck top: Step 5a.

b.   With right sides together and markings matched, pin ribbing to waist area. With ribbing on top, stitch, stretching ribbing to fit between markings. If a straight stitch is used, sew a backup row of stitches just inside the front row. Press seam toward body of top.

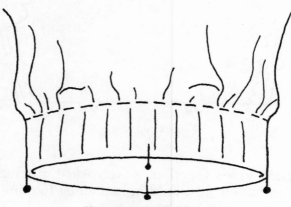

V-neck top: Step 5b.

6.   Work sleeve as follows:
a.   Ease-stitch upper sleeve between notches. Clean-finish (edgestitch) lower sleeve if fabric ravels.

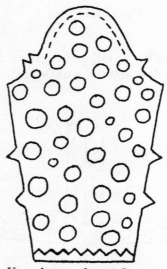

V-neck top, sleeve: Step 6a.

118

b. Pin and stitch sleeve seam. Press. Pin and blindstitch sleeve hem. Press.

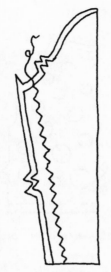

V-neck top: Step 6b.

7. With right sides together, pin sleeve in armhole, matching symbols and underarm seams. Adjust ease and stitch. (Use two rows of stitching if straight stitch is used.) Trim and press seam toward sleeve.

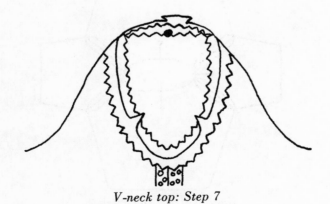

V-neck top: Step 7

RAGLAN-SLEEVE TOP WITH NECK, WAIST, AND SLEEVE RIBBING

1. Staystitch front and back neckline and lower edge.

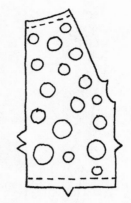

Raglan-sleeve top: Step 1.

2. Pin and stitch sleeve to front and back armhole edges. If using a straight stitch, reinforce lower end of armhole with a backup row of stitches. Clip and press seams.

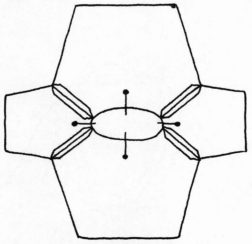

Raglan-sleeve top: Step 2.

3.   Stitch ribbing together to form a tube. With right sides together, fold neck ribbing lengthwise. Mark and divide into four equal parts.

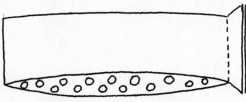

Raglan-sleeve top: Step 3a.

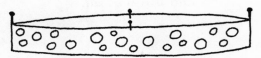

Raglan-sleeve top: Step 3b.

4.   Mark and divide neck area into four equal parts. With right sides together and markings matched, pin ribbing to neck area. Stitch with ribbing on top, stretching ribbing to fit between markings. Press seam toward body of garment.

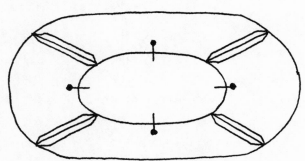

Raglan-sleeve top: Step 4a.

121

Raglan-sleeve top: Step 4b.

5. Pin and stitch front to back at sides and sleeves. Stitch in one continuous seam. Clip and press seam.

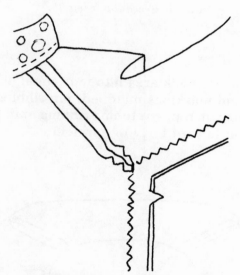

Raglan-sleeve top: Step 5.

6. Apply (a) sleeve and (b) waist ribbing same as for neck.

122

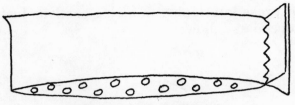

Raglan-sleeve top: Step 6a.

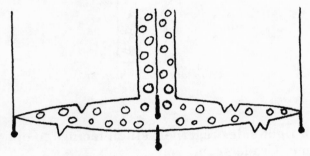

Raglan-sleeve top: Step 6b.

TAB-FRONT DRESS USING OPEN-SLEEVE METHOD

1.   Reinforce front opening by stitching along seamline, pivoting at corners. Clip corners.

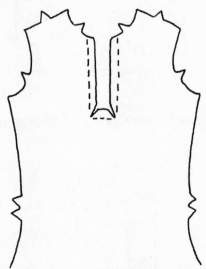

Tab-front dress: Step 1.

2. Baste or press interfacing to facing sections just inside the foldline. Proceed as follows:

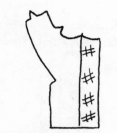

Tab-front dress: Step 2.

a. With right sides together, stitch facings to opening along stitching line. Grade seam.

Tab-front dress: Step 2a.

b. Fold and press facings along foldline to inside of garment.

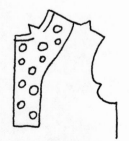

Tab-front dress: Step 2b.

c.   Position right facing over left. Stitch through facings and wedge.

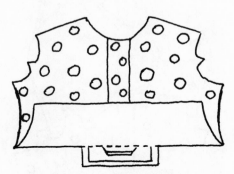

Tab-front dress: Step 2c.

3.   Pin and stitch front to back at shoulder seams. Press.

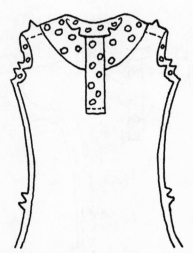

Tab-front dress: Step 3.

4.   With right sides together, position sleeve in armhole, matching notches. Stitch.

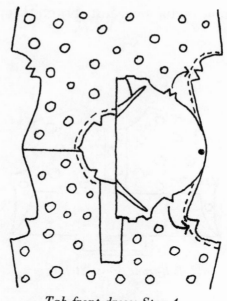

Tab-front dress: Step 4.

5. With right sides together, pin and stitch side seams and sleeve seams in one continuous operation.

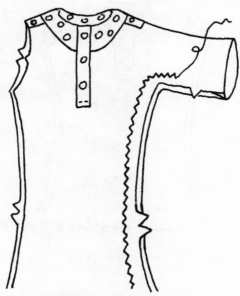

Tab-front dress: Step 5.

6. Construct and position collar as follows:

a. Baste interfacing to wrong side of undercollar. Trim interfacing.

Tab-front dress: Step 6a.

b. With fusible interfacing, press to wrong side of upper collar, inside seamlines.

Tab-front dress: Step 6b.

c. With right sides together, stitch collar sections together, leaving neck edge open. Grade seams. Clip. Trim corners. Turn and press.

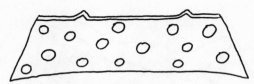

Tab-front dress; Step 6c.

d. Pin collar to neck edge, matching symbols. Clip neck edge if necessary and baste.

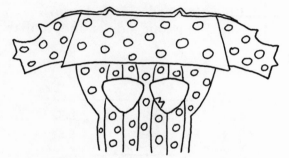

Tab-front dress: Step 6d.

7. Apply facing as follows:
    a. Staystitch neck edge of back facing.

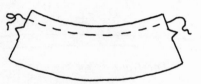

Tab-front dress: Step 7a.

   b. Stitch to front facings at shoulders. Trim and press seams.

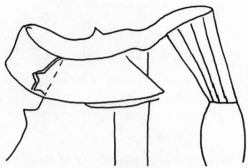

Tab-front dress: Step 7b.

c.   With right sides together and facing folded on front fold-lines, pin and stitch facing to neck edge. Clip where necessary. Understitch back facing to back seam allowance close to seam. Grade seams and press away from collar.

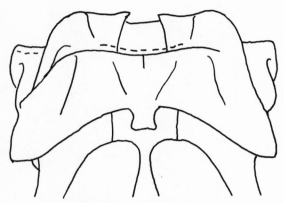

Tab-front dress: Step 7c.

d.   Turn facing rightside out, observing foldlines. Press. Tack to shoulder by hand or stitch in the ditch.

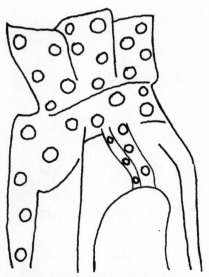

Tab-front dress: Step 7d.

8. Hem by machine or hand blindstitch. An acceptable width is 1½ to 3 inches or less than 3 inches if skirt is full. If knit is not heavy, you can use narrow fusible tape.

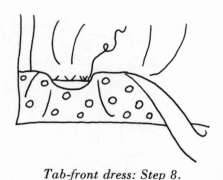

Tab-front dress: Step 8.

SCOOP-NECK JUMPER WITH FOLDOVER BRAID

1. Staystitch neckline, front and back, and armhole edges.

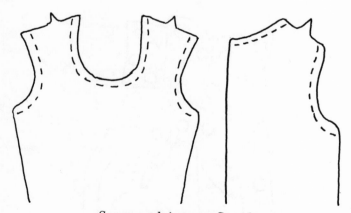

Scoop-neck jumper: Step 1.

2. Stitch front to back at shoulder seams. Trim and press.

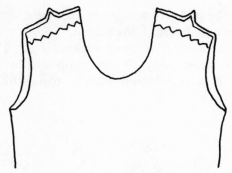

Scoop-neck jumper: Step 2.

3. To apply braid proceed as follows:
    a. Press braid open.

Scoop-neck jumper: Step 3a.

    b. If there is no opening in garment, seam ends of braid, forming a circle; if there is an opening in garment, raw edge of braid should be even with raw edge of garment.

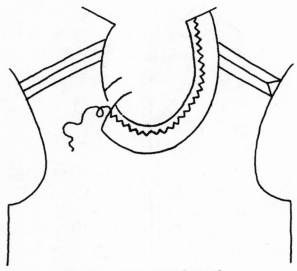

Scoop-neck jumper: Step 3b.

c. Pin one edge of braid along seamline on wrong side of neck edge. Stitch close to edge. Clip curve.

4. Turn trim to outside over neck edge. Press. Pin trim to neck, stretching where necessary to maintain curve. Stitch close to edge of trim with a regulation stitch, topstitch, or decorative stitch. Press.

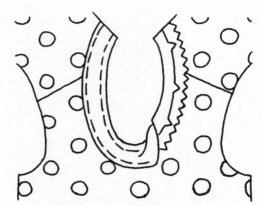

Scoop-neck jumper: Step 4.

5. Stitch center back seam to bottom of closure opening. Press seam open. Apply zipper in the usual manner. A hook and eye can be used at the top if desired.

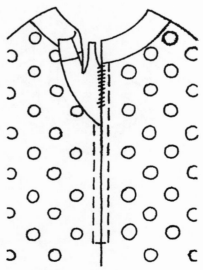

Scoop-neck jumper: Step 5.

6. Apply armhole braid in same manner as for neckline.

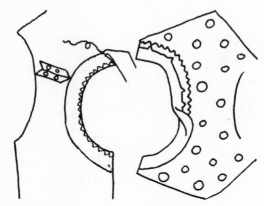

Scoop-neck jumper: Step 6.

7. With right sides together, stitch front to back at side seams. Clip seam where necessary. Press. Slipstitch upper ends of side seam and center back seam.

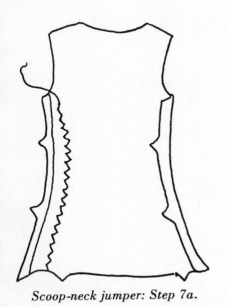

Scoop-neck jumper: Step 7a.

Scoop-neck jumper: Step 7b.

8. Hem with blind stitch or fusible hemming tape.

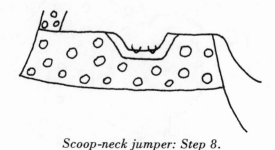

Scoop-neck jumper: Step 8.

SLACKS WITH ELASTIC WAISTBAND

1. Construct pant legs as follows:

    a. With right sides together, pin pants front to back at side seams. Stitch directionally. Press open if ⅝ inch seam; press to one side if ¼ inch seam.

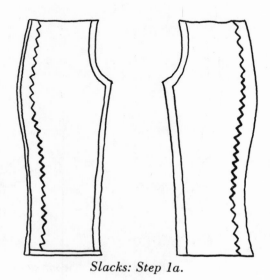

Slacks: Step 1a.

b. With right sides together, pin and stitch inside seams. Press.

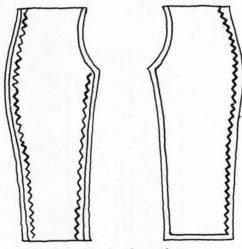

Slacks: Step 1b.

c. Turn rightside out. To stitch-in front crease use a single or a double needle. When using a single needle, proceed as follows: Stitch a very narrow seam directionally at the crease line, through double thickness. Using the double-needle method, change to double needle and raised seam foot. Tighten tension. Stitch directionally. (This method can be employed only when the pant fronts are unattached, as stitching is done through a single thickness.) Position pant leg with inside seam over outside seam. Press in front crease to top of pant leg. Press back crease to height of crotch. To permanently crease pants, use the white vinegar method detailed earlier in the section on pressing.

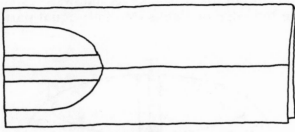

Slacks: Step 1c.

135

2.   Place one pant leg rightside out, and inside of other pant leg wrongside out. Place inside seams together and pin entire crotch seam. Use a triple-lock stretch stitch or a double row of zigzag or straight stitches, the second row being ⅛ inch from the first. Clip where necessary. Press seam.

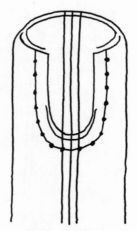

Slacks: Step 2.

3.   To prepare elastic proceed as follows:
   a.   Lap waistline elastic ½ inch, forming a circle, and stitch.
   b.   Mark and pin elastic into four parts.

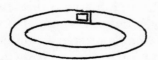

Slacks: Step 3a.

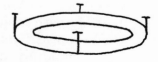

Slacks: Step 3b.

4.   Attach elastic to top of slacks as follows:
   a.   Divide top edge of slacks into four equal parts.

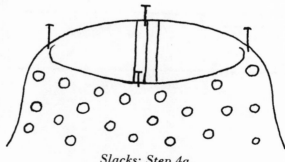

Slacks: Step 4a.

b.   Matching marked divisions, pin elastic to wrong side of pants, top edges even. With elastic on top, stretch and stitch elastic to fit between markings, using a stretch or zigzag stitch.

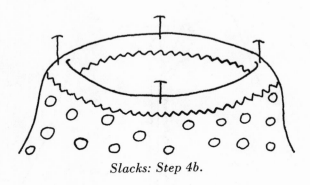

Slacks: Step 4b.

c.   Turn elastic and fabric over once and stitch again.

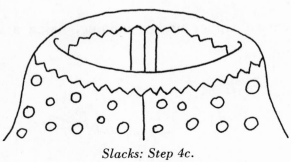

Slacks: Step 4c.

5.   Hem lower pant leg with a 1½ inch hem. Blindstitch or fuse in place. For a mock-French or conventional cuff, refer to Part 2.

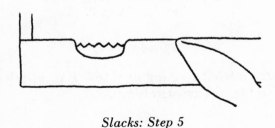

Slacks: Step 5

A-LINE SKIRT WITH CONVENTIONAL WAISTBAND

1. Pin and stitch center back sections to closure opening. Press seam.

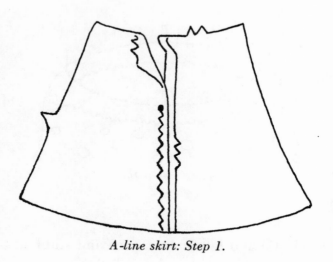

A-line skirt: Step 1.

2. Apply closed zipper under opening, using a zipper foot. Stitch.

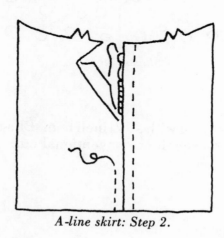

A-line skirt: Step 2.

3. Pin and stitch front to back at sides. Easestitch upper opening of skirt. (Refer to easestitching).

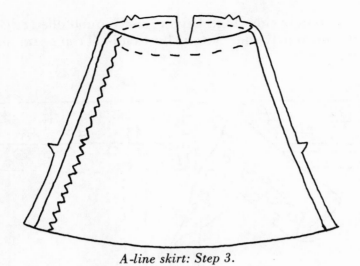

A-line skirt: Step 3.

4. Baste or fuse interfacing to wrong side of waistband. Turn and press under seam allowance on long, unnotched side.

A-line skirt: Step 4.

5. Attach waistband to skirt as follows:
    a.   With right sides together, and symbols and notches matching, ease and pin waistband to upper edge of skirt. Stitch. Grade seam. Press toward waistband.

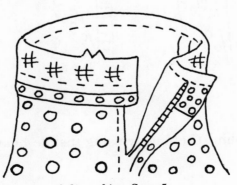

A-line skirt: Step 5a.

b. With right sides together and short, unnotched edges even, fold and pin waistband. Stitch short ends. Trim seam and seam corners.

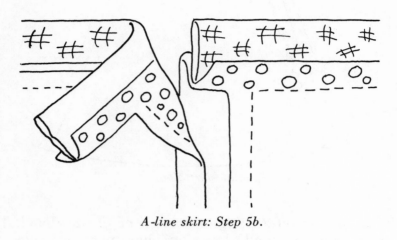

A-line skirt: Step 5b.

c. Turn and position unstitched edge just below previous stitching line. Press and pin. On outside of the waistband, stitch in the ditch to secure the inner waistband.

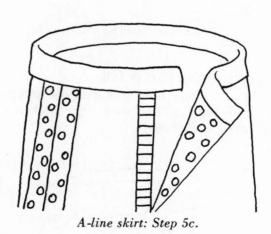

A-line skirt: Step 5c.

6. Hem by blindstitching or using fusible hemming tape.

140

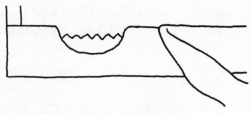

A-line skirt: Step 6.

MULTIPLE-GORED SKIRT WITH ELASTIC WAISTBAND

1.   With wrong sides together, fold lengthwise and press crease into each gore.

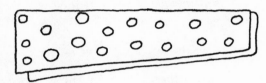

Multiple-gored skirt: Step 1.

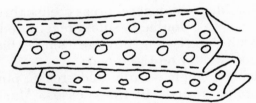

Multiple-gored skirt: Steps 2 and 3.

2.   Assemble gores as follows:
     a.   Right sides together, stitch all gores together using a knit, zigzag, or straight stitch and a ¼ inch seam allowance. Press seams open or to one side.

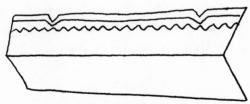

Multiple-gored skirt: Step 2a.

b. Clip all seams (¾) three-fourth inches from the top (preferred elastic width), and width of hem from the bottom.

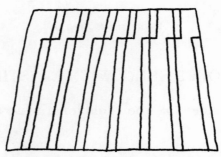

Multiple-gored skirt: Step 2b.

c. Press seam allowances open in these areas or opposite those already pressed. Pin or tape hem in position.
3. Stitch raised seam in each gore as follows:
a. On the outside of each gore, press crease through all thicknesses. To stitch with a double needle, crease need not be folded or pinned in, as stitching is done through a single thickness except for hem. Tension should be tightened.
b. When using a single needle, fold crease, pin, and stitch a very narrow seam through all thicknesses. Maintain tension. Using either method, no further stitching is needed on the hem.

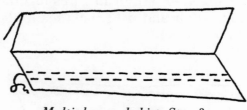

Multiple-gored skirt: Step 3.

4. Attach elastic to waistline as follows:

a.   Stitch short elastic ends together and divide into fourths.

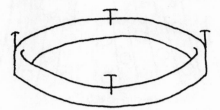

Multiple-gored skirt: Step 4a.

b.   Also divide upper portion of skirt. Position elastic even with upper edges on wrong side of skirt. Match and pin divisions. With elastic on top, use a stretch or zigzag stitch while stretching and stitching elastic in place.

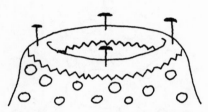

Multiple-gored skirt: Step 4b.

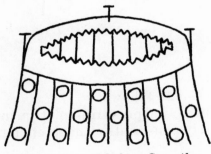

Multiple-gored skirt: Step 4b.

c.   Fold band over once and stitch again.

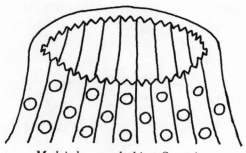

Multiple-gored skirt: Step 4c.

CARDIGAN WITH RAGLAN SLEEVES

1. With right sides together, pin and stitch sleeve to cardigan front and back at shoulder seams. Press seams.

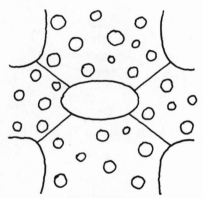

Cardigan: Step 1.

2. For trim proceed as follows:

    a. Fold lengthwise and press rib-knit trim in half. Trim should equal approximately two-thirds of neck opening.

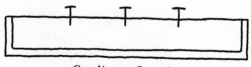

144   *Cardigan: Step 2a.*

b.   Divide and mark trim and neck into quarters. Pin accordingly. Stitch with trim on top, stretching trim to fit between markings. Press seam away from trim.

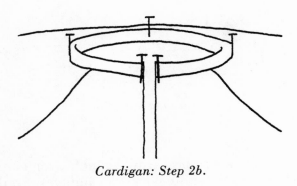

Cardigan: Step 2b.

3.   Stitch rib trim to lower edge of sleeve in like manner.

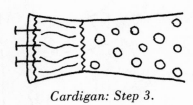

Cardigan: Step 3.

4.   With right sides together, stitch side and underarm seams in one continuous seam. If using a straight stitch, stretch while stitching.

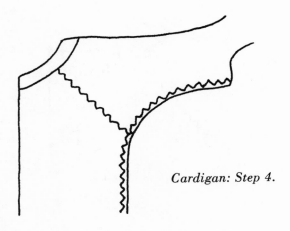

Cardigan: Step 4.

5. Pin bottom hem in place. Stitch with blindstitch. Press.

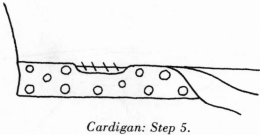

Cardigan: Step 5.

6. On right side, lap ribbon trim ¼ inch over cardigan front opening, with ½ inch extending over top and bottom edges. Press trim to wrong side and slipstitch.

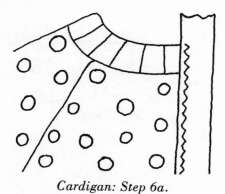

Cardigan: Step 6a.

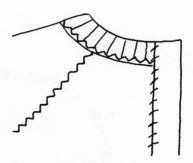

Cardigan: Step 6b.

7.   Work vertical corded buttonholes, right side for women, left side for men. Sew buttons on the opposite side.

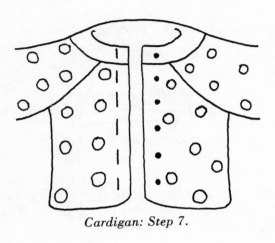

Cardigan: Step 7.

BLAZER JACKET WITH SET-IN SLEEVES AND CUT-ON FACINGS

1.   Stitch darts in jacket front and back. Press bust darts down and others toward center.

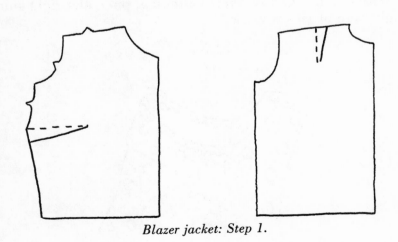

Blazer jacket: Step 1.

2.   Make bound buttonholes on jacket front according to directions given in Part 2 under "Buttonholes."
3.   With right sides together and notches matching, stitch jacket front to back at shoulder and side seams. Press seams. Clip where necessary.
4.   Stitch or fuse interfacing to collar. Trim.

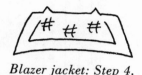

Blazer jacket: Step 4.

5.   With right sides together, join upper collar to lower collar, leaving neck edge open. Grade or bevel seam. Turn and press, rolling seam toward the under collar.

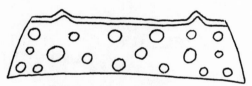

Blazer jacket: Step 5.

6.   With notches and symbols matching, pin collar right side up to right side of jacket neck.

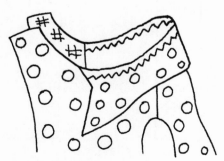

Blazer jacket: Step 6.

7. Join back neck facing to front facing at shoulder seam. Trim seam.

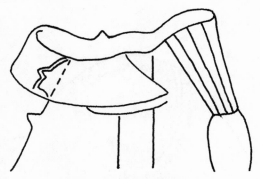

Blazer jacket: Step 7.

8. With right sides together, notches and symbols matching, and front facing folded on foldline, stitch entire neck. Grade or bevel seam. Clip where necessary. Turn and press.

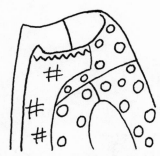

Blazer jacket: Step 8.

9. With right sides together, pin and stitch underarm sleeve seams. Press.

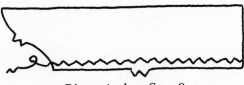

Blazer jacket: Step 9.

10. With right sides together and symbols and notches matching, pin sleeve to armhole. With sleeve on bottom, stretch and
stitch sleeve armhole to fit between markings. Trim seam. Clip
where necessary. Press seam toward sleeve.

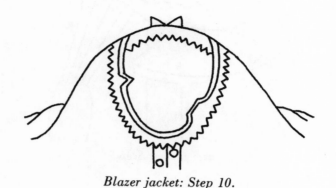

Blazer jacket: Step 10.

11. Hem jacket as follows:
   a. Open out facing at lower edge of jacket. Turn up hem.
Secure with blindstitch, catchstitch, or fusible hemming tape.

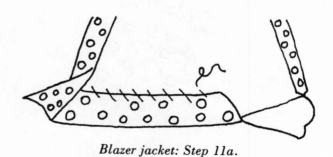

Blazer jacket: Step 11a.

   b. Turn facing to inside along foldline and slipstitch to hem.
Press.

150

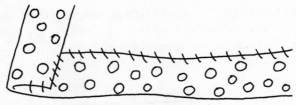

Blazer jacket: Step 11b.

12.   On outside of jacket, stitch in the ditch (depression) around each buttonhole. On wrong side of jacket, trim fabric from within stitching lines. If machine buttonholes are to be used, make them now through jacket front and facing.
13.   Sew buttons to opposite side of jacket front. Press entire jacket.

BODY SHIRT WITH CUT ON FACINGS

1.   With right sides together, pin and stitch front and back darts. Press bust darts down, others toward center.

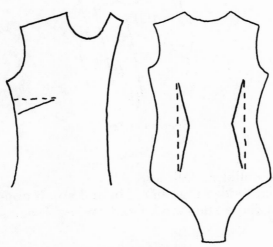

Body shirt: Step 1.

2.   Stitch or fuse interfacing to wrong side of front facing, upper collar, and under collar stand (lower portion of under collar). Stitch along foldline of undercollar.

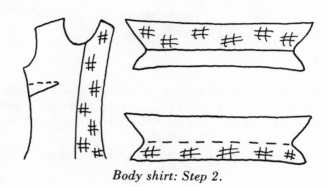

Body shirt: Step 2.

3.   With right sides together, join front to back at shoulder seams.

Body shirt Step 3.

4.   Assemble collar as follows:
   a.   With right sides together, pin and stitch upper collar and stand to under collar and stand. Grade or bevel seams. Clip where indicated.

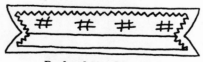

Body shirt: Step 4a.

152

b.   Turn collar. Press while rolling seam toward under collar.

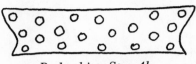

Body shirt: Step 4b.

5.   Pin and stitch collar (rightside up) to neck edge, matching notches and symbols.

Body shirt: Step 5.

6.   Attach front facings and collar seam allowance as follows:
   a.   Fold facing on foldlines over upper collar to shoulder. Stitch on stitching line. Grade or bevel seams. Turn to right side. Stitch collar seam allowance between shoulders to stitching line below. Secure facings to inside shoulder seams with a few hand or machine stitches.

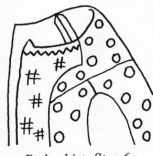

Body shirt: Step 6a.

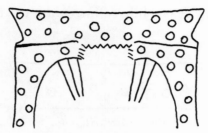

Body shirt: Step 6b.

7.   Construct sleeve as follows:
    a.   With right sides together, pin and stitch sleeve underarm seam. Press. Turn up lower edge of sleeve along foldline. Stitch on stitching line, leaving a one-inch opening. Insert elastic through opening and secure ends. Slipstitch opening.

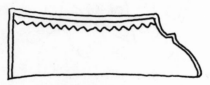

Body shirt: Step 7a.

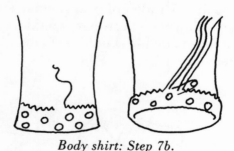

Body shirt: Step 7b.

8.   With right sides together, pin sleeve to armhole, matching symbols and seams. Stitch with sleeve on bottom, stretching sleeve opening to fit. Trim. Clip where necessary. Above notches, press seam toward sleeve.

154

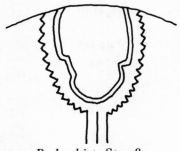

Body shirt: Step 8.

9. Construct crotch as follows:
    a. With right sides together, stitch center front crotch seam to indicated symbol. Press.

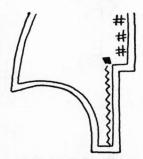

Body shirt: Step 9a.

    b. Above crotch seamline, fold right facing wrongside out along foldline. Stitch from foldline to crotch seamline. Clip. Trim seam. Turn rightside out and press.

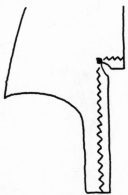

Body shirt: Step 9b.

c.   Clip to symbol on left side of crotch seam. Press entire length of fold.

d.   Position right front over left front at center symbol. Top-stitch from center symbol to seamline.

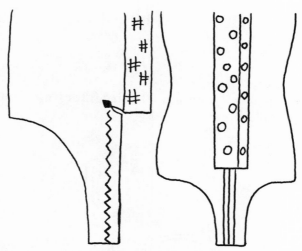

Body shirt: Steps 9c and 9d.

10.   With right sides together, pin and stitch side seams directionally. Press.

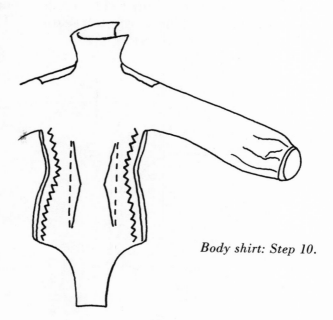

Body shirt: Step 10.

11.   Pin and stitch elastic, as previously described, to outside leg area, stretching elastic and using wide zigzag stitch. Turn and stitch again.

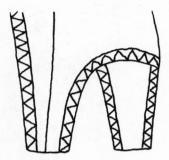

Body shirt: Step 11.

12.   Finish crotch as follows:
  a.   Apply ¾ inch interfacing to ends of crotch on wrong side. Turn and zigzag stitch.

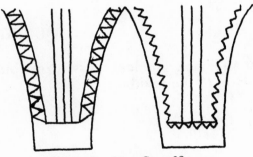

Body shirt: Step 12a.

  b.   Attach gripper snaps according to manufacturer's instructions.

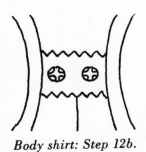

Body shirt: Step 12b.

13.　Work vertical buttonholes on right front. Sew buttons on left front.

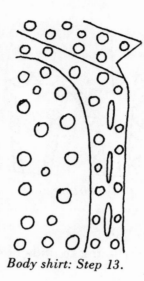

Body shirt: Step 13.

QUICKIE JUMPSUIT

1.　Stitch bust and back shoulder darts. Press bust darts down, and shoulder darts to the middle.

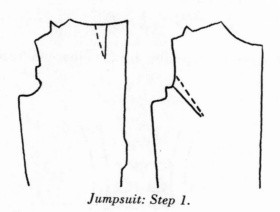

Jumpsuit: Step 1.

2. Stitch or fuse interfacing to wrong side of neck edges. Trim close to seamline.

Jumpsuit: Step 2.

3. With right sides together, stitch center front seams to point of closure. Press. Apply zipper to front center opening according to manufacturer's instructions, or refer to zippers in Part 2.

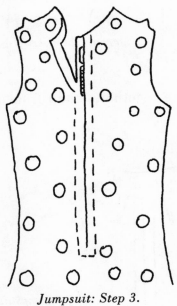

Jumpsuit: Step 3.

4. With right sides together and notches matching, stitch center back seam. Press.

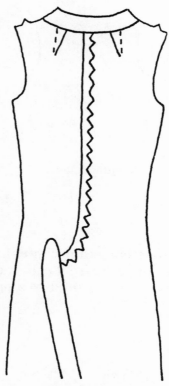

Jumpsuit: Step 4.

5. With right sides together, stitch front to back at shoulder seams. Press.

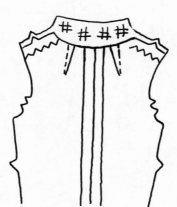

Jumpsuit: Step 5.

6. Apply facings as follows:
   a. Join facings at shoulder seams. Press and trim.

Jumpsuit: Step 6a.

   b. With right sides together, notches and seams matching, stitch facing to neck area.

Jumpsuit: Step 6b.

   c. Understitch facing to seam allowance close to stitching line. Trim seam. Clip where necessary.

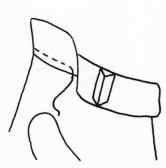

Jumpsuit: Step 6c.

d.   Slipstitch turned facing edges to zipper tape on fronts. Stitch facing to shoulder seams.

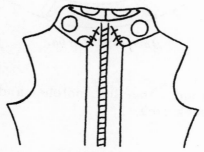

Jumpsuit: Step 6d.

7.   Construct sleeve as follows:
   a.   With notches matching, stitch underarm seam. Press.

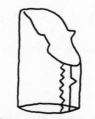

Jumpsuit: Step 7a.

   b.   With right sides together, notches and shoulder seams matching, pin sleeve to armhole. With sleeve on bottom, stitch, stretching sleeve armhole to fit. Trim seam. Clip where necessary. Press seam toward sleeve.

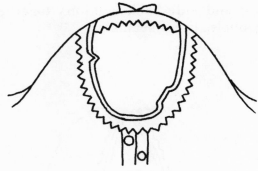

Jumpsuit: Step 7b.

8.   Turn up lower sleeve and pant legs. Slipstitch or fuse in place.

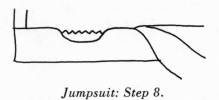

Jumpsuit: Step 8.

CAPE WITH MANDARIN COLLAR AND BUTTON LOOPS

1.   With right sides together and notches matching, pin and stitch front and side sections together. Leave opening between indicated symbols for arm slits. Press seams.

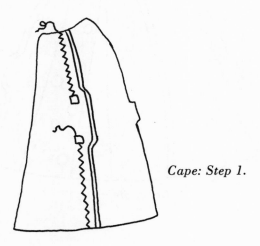

Cape: Step 1.

2. Stitch back and side-back sections together, matching notches and symbols. Press seams.

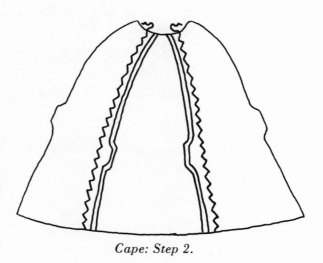

Cape: Step 2.

3. With right sides together, stitch front to back at shoulder side seams. Press.

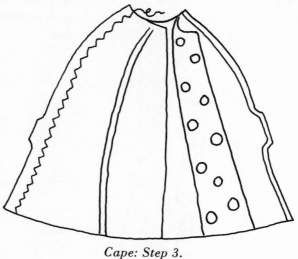

Cape: Step 3.

164

4. Assemble and attach collar as follows:
   a. Stitch or fuse interfacing to upper collar.

Cape collar: Step 4a.

b. With right sides together, join collar sections, leaving neck edge open. Trim seam. Turn to the outside. Press collar, rolling seam to the underside.

Cape collar: Step 4b.

c. Position collar (rightside up) on right side of neck, matching notches and symbols. Stitch. Trim seam. Clip curve where necessary.

Cape collar: Step 4c.

5.   Construct and attach button loops as follows:
   a.   Cut a bias strip of fabric one inch wide and fold in half lengthwise, right sides together. Stitch a narrow seam.

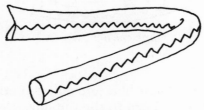

Cape, button loops: Step 5a.

   b.   Attach needle and thread through one end of strip. Work through tube, turning strip to the right side.

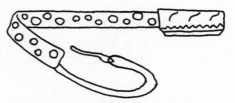

Cape, button loops: Step 5b.

   c.   Cut bias into ⅝ inch sections.

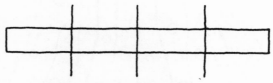

Cape, button loops: Step 5c.

   d.   Pin and stitch strips to right front. Sew buttons to left front.

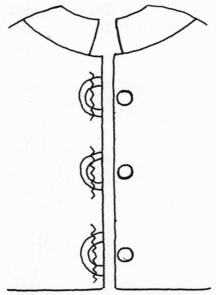

Cape, buttons and loops: Step 5d.

6. With right sides together, pin and stitch facings to right front and neck. Stitch. Trim seam. Turn to right side. Press, rolling seam slightly to the underside.

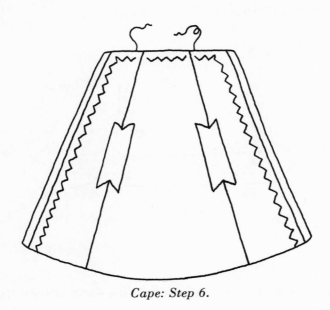

Cape: Step 6.

7.   Topstitch collar and front slits as illustrated. With a needle thread loose ends and bring to the wrong side and knot.

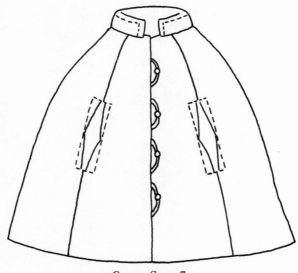

Cape: Step 7.

8.   Hem as follows:
    a.   Turn up hem. Open out facings at lower edge of front cape. Secure with blindstitch or fuse in place.

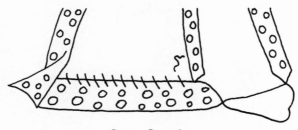

Cape: Step 8a.

    b.   Turn facing to inside along foldlines and slipstitch. Press.

168

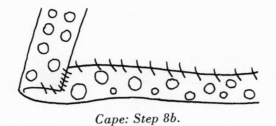

Cape: Step 8b.

WRAP ROBE

1.   Construct front bodice as follows:
     a.   Stitch or fuse interfacing to wrong side of bodice front sections. Trim to seamline. With right sides together, fold ties along foldlines.

Wrap robe: Step 1a.

   b.   Stitch long edge and straight end. Grade or bevel seam.

Wrap robe: Step 1b.

c. Turn to the right side. Press.

Wrap robe: Step 1c.

d. Pin ties to right side of bodice fronts, on indicated markings. Stitch.

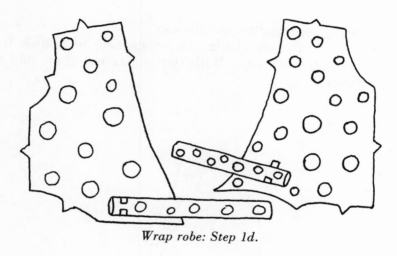

Wrap robe: Step 1d.

2. Pin and stitch darts in bodice front and back. Press toward center.

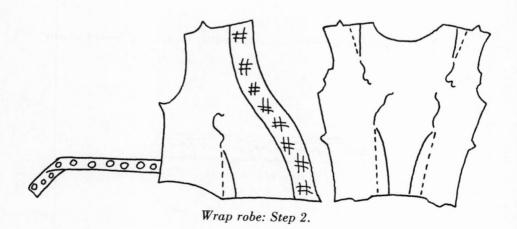

Wrap robe: Step 2.

3.   With right sides together, pin and stitch bodice shoulder and side seams. Press.

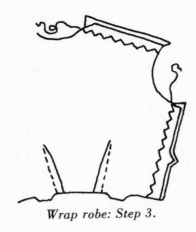

Wrap robe: Step 3.

4.   Assemble collar as follows:
   a.   Stitch or fuse interfacing to upper collar. Trim close to stitching line.

Wrap robe: Step 4a.

   b.   With right sides together, notches and symbols matching, pin and stitch collar sections together, leaving neck edge open.
   c.   Turn and press seamline slightly to the underside of collar.

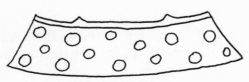

Wrap robe: Step 4c.

171

5. Attach facing and collar as follows:

    a.   With right sides together, join bodice back facing to front facing at shoulder seams. Trim seam. Press.

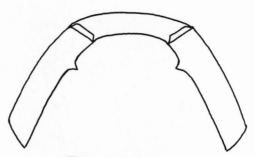

Wrap robe: Step 5a.

    b.   Pin collar, rightside up, to outside of bodice neck, matching notches and symbols.

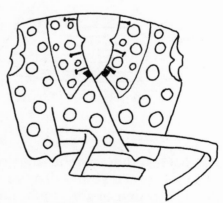

Wrap robe: Step 5b.

    c.   With right sides together, notches and symbols matching, pin facing to collar and neck edge. Stitch through all thicknesses.

172

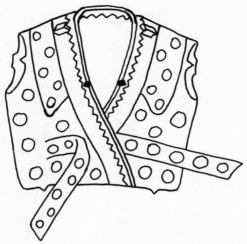

Wrap robe: Step 5c.

d. Understitch facing to seam allowance. Grade or bevel seams. Clip where necessary. Turn and press.

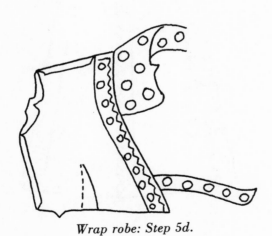

Wrap robe: Step 5d.

6. Stitch skirt as follows:

    a. Right sides together and notches matching, pin and stitch center back seam. Press

Wrap robe: Step 6a.

b.   Join skirt fronts to back at side seams. Press.

Wrap robe: Step 6b.

174

7. Attach skirt to bodice as follows:

   a. With right sides together, notches matching, and folding facing out, pin skirt to bodice. With skirt on bottom and bodice on top, stitch, stretching bodice to fit between notches. Press seam up.

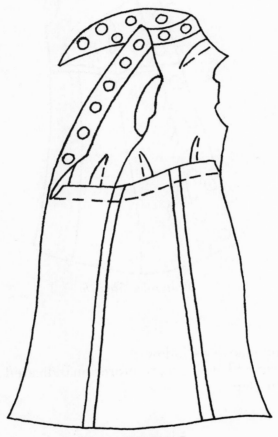

Wrap robe: Step 7a.

b. Fold self-facing on skirt fronts to the inside. Blindstitch or slipstitch to within six inches of hem. Press. Lap right front over left. Attach hook and eye where indicated.

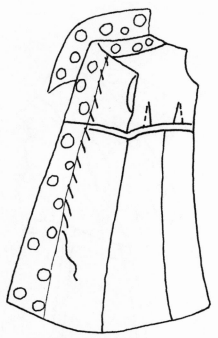

Wrap robe: Step 7b.

8. Construct sleeve as follows:
     a. At lower end of sleeve, reinforce on indicated stitching line for continuous lap.

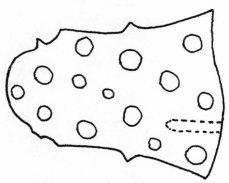

Wrap robe: Step 8a.

b. Cut between lines of stitching.

Wrap robe: Step 8b.

c. Cut two strips of self-fabric the full length of the cut area and 1½ inches in width.
Position the cut area flat. With right sides together, pin facing to slashed area. Stitch outside the previous stitching line. Grade seam. Press away from sleeve.

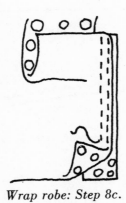

Wrap robe: Step 8c.

d. Press under ¼ inch on opposite edge of facing. Position over previous stitching. Slipstitch.

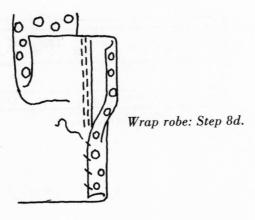

Wrap robe: Step 8d.

e.   Turn front edge of lap to inside. Baste lower edge.

Wrap robe: Step 8e.

f.   Stitch sleeve seam. Press.
Stitch a row of gathering stitches at lower edge of sleeve, between laps.

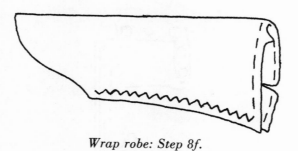

Wrap robe: Step 8f.

9.   Assemble and stitch cuff as follows:
a.   Stitch or fuse interfacing to cuff between foldline and notched edge. Press seam allowance on unnotched edge to the wrong side.

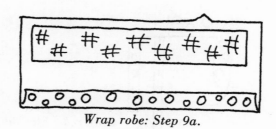

Wrap robe: Step 9a.

b. With right sides together, pin notched edge of cuff to sleeve, matching notches and symbols. Stitch. Grade and press seam toward cuff.

Wrap robe: Step 9b.

c. Turn and press cuff along foldline. Stitch in place by slip-stitching or stitching in the ditch. Make machine or bound buttonholes where directed. Attach buttons where indicated.

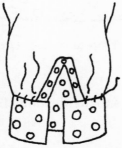

Wrap robe: Step 9c.

10. With right sides together, notches and symbols matching, pin sleeve in armhole. Stitch with sleeve on bottom, stretching armhole where necessary. Grade and clip seam. Press seam toward sleeve.

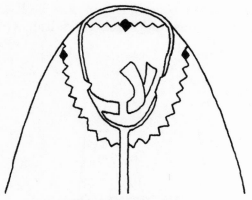

Wrap robe: Step 10.

11.   Hem as follows:
     a.   Open front facings outward at lower edge of skirt. Turn up hem. Secure with blindstitch or use fusible hemming tape.

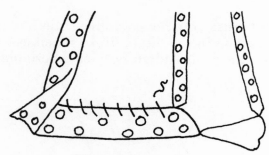

Wrap robe: Step 11a.

     b.   Turn front facings to inside along foldlines and slipstitch to hem. Press.

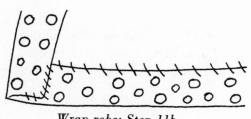

Wrap robe: Step 11b.

180

1. Assemble front with lace as follows:
    a. Stitch darts in front. Press down.

Slip: Step 1a.

b. With right sides together, pin lace to upper portion of slip, making decorative edge even with raw edge.

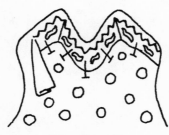

Slip: Step 1b.

c. Miter and pin lace to center front and at points.

Slip: Step 1c.

d.   Unpin lace. Stitch miters on wrong side of lace with a fine zigzag, straight, or knit stitch. Trim close to seam. Press. (If using a straight stitch, make a backup row of stitches.)

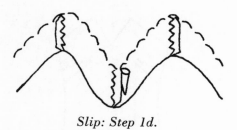

Slip: Step 1d.

e.   Repin right side of lace to right side of slip, having decorative edges even with raw edges of slip. Stitch close to straight edge.

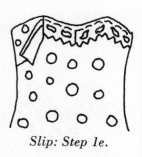

Slip: Step 1e.

f.   Trim away slip close to stitching line. Press seam down toward slip. Stitch again over stitching line, on outside of slip.

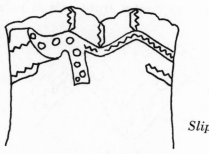

Slip: Step 1f.

g. Pin right side of lace to lower right slip edge, making decorative edge even with raw edge. Stitch close to straight edge.

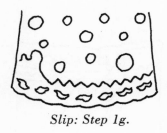

Slip: Step 1g.

h. Trim close to stitching line. Press trimmed edge toward slip and stitch again over stitching line on outside of slip.

Slip: Step 1h.

2. Attach lace to upper back section as follows:

a. Pin right side of lace to right side of upper back section, keeping decorative edge even with raw edge. Stitch close to straight edge.

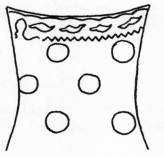

Slip: Step 2a.

b. Trim close to stitching line. Press seam toward slip and stitch again over stitching line on outside of slip. Pin and stitch lace to lower edge of back, as for front.

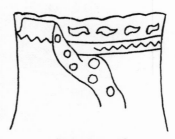

Slip: Step 2b.

3. Stitch front to back at side seams. Press.

Slip: Step 3.

4. Cut two pieces of ribbon to fit comfortably over shoulders from front to back. Adjust and pin on indicated symbols. Stitch.

Slip: Step 4.

PANTIES

1. Attach front and back to crotch as follows:
   a. Staystitch lower edges of front and back. Clip where necessary.

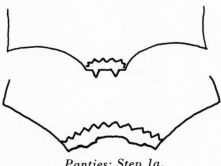

Panties: Step 1a.

b. With right sides together, notches and symbols matching, pin and stitch crotch to front and back. Trim seam. Press toward crotch.

Panties: Step 1b.

c. Press under seam allowance on notched edges of remaining crotch section.

Panties: Step 1c.

d. Pin right side of second crotch section against wrong side of back.
Stitch and trim seam. Press toward crotch. With wrong sides together, pin remaining crotch edge to front section. Machine or handstitch over stitching line. Press.

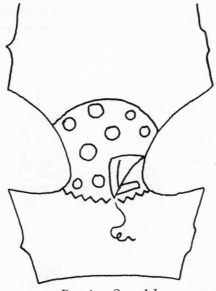

Panties: Step 1d.

2. Apply elastic to leg as follows:

    a.   Cut two pieces of lingerie elastic two inches smaller than leg measurement or fit to leg for comfort. Divide and mark elastic and leg edges into eight equal parts. On inside, pin elastic to leg edges along seamline. With elastic on top, stitch, stretching where necessary for fit. Trim seam.

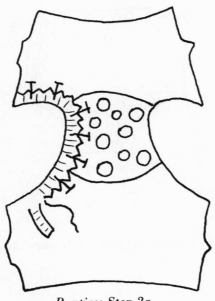

Panties: Step 2a.

b.   Turn elastic to the outside and pin matching markings. Stitch close to the elastic edge, stretching where necessary.

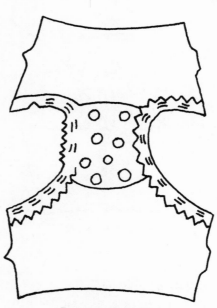

Panties: Step 2b.

c.   Stitch front to back at one side seam. Trim and press.

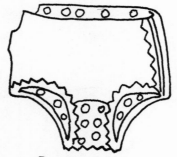

Panties: Step 2c.

3.   Cut a ½ inch lingerie elastic 2 inches smaller than waist

measurement. Divide and mark elastic and waistline of panties into 8 equal parts. Pin elastic to wrong side of wasitline, matching markings and edges. Stitch, stretching where necessary. Turn stitched area over once and stitch again. Stitch remaining side seam. Trim and press.

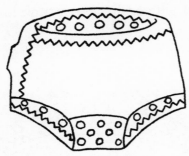

Panties: Step 3.

BRA

1.   Assemble front bra sections as follows:
    a.   Stitch darts in front. Trim and press open. Stitch center front seam. Trim and press. Press under seam allowance on back edges. Stitch a ¼ inch seam. Trim close to seamline.

Bra: Step 1a.

    b.   Stitch bra facings same as for front sections. With right sides together, pin facing to bra, matching center front seams. Stitch along upper edge. Trim seam. Clip where necessary.

Bra: Step 1b.

c.   Turn to right side and press. Stitch lower edges together along seamline.

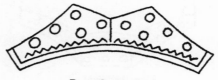

Bra: Step 1c.

d.   Trim sections of purchased closure kit to fit between open back edges of bra and facing.

Bra: Step 1d.

e.   Attach closures according to manufacturer's directions.

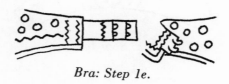

Bra: Step 1e.

2.   Complete bra as follows:
   a.   Cut lingerie elastic two inches smaller than lower edge of

bra. Mark center. On inside, pin elastic to lower edge of bra along seam line, matching centers. Stitch, stretching elastic to extend ¼ inch at back edges. Trim close to stitching line.

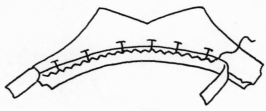

Bra: Step 2a.

b.   Turn and pin elastic to outside, being careful to pin under ¼ inch at back edges. Stitch close to elastic edge, stretching where necessary.

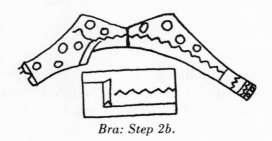

Bra: Step 2b.

c.   Pin and stitch purchased shoulder straps to inside on indicated markings. Adjust to fit.

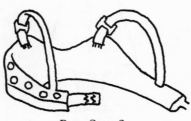

Bra: Step 2c.

1.   With right sides together, notches and symbols matching, stitch center back seam. Use stretch or zigzag stitch, or a double row of straight stitches. (If using a straight stitch, stretch fabric while stitching.)

Swimsuit, center-back seam: Step 1.

2.   Attach crotch as follows:
    a.   With right sides together and symbols matching, stitch crotch and lining to back in a single seam.

Swimsuit, crotch: Step 2a.

b.   Stitch crotch and lining to front pant section, with right sides together and symbols matching.

Swimsuit, crotch and pant section: Step 2b.

3.   With right sides together and notches matching, stitch side front sections to front. Fold under and stitch indicated hem on front.

Swimsuit, side-front section: Step 3.

4.   Stitch swimsuit elastic to leg openings, following same procedure as for panties.

Swimsuit, elastic leg openings: Step 4.

5.   With right sides together, pin back to front at side seams. Position pants panel, rightside down, over front, observing specified markings. Stitch through all thicknesses in a single seam. Trim and slipstitch lower end of seams.

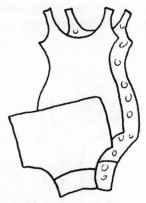

Swimsuit, pants panel and side seams: Step 5.

6.   With right sides together, stitch front to back at shoulder seams.

194

Swimsuit, shoulder seams: Step 6.

7.   Stitch elastic ends together to form a circle. Divide and mark as previously described. Position and pin to neckline. Stitch, stretching where necessary. Fold over and stitch again.

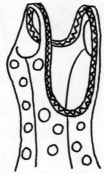

Swimsuit, elastic neckline: Step 7.

8.   For arm openings, stitch elastic ends together to form a circle. Divide, mark, and position. Stitch, stretching where necessary. Fold over and stitch again.

195

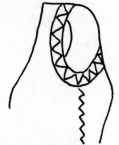

Swimsuit, arm openings: Step 8.

9.   Pin bra cups in place. Secure at top and side seams.

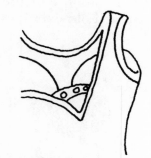

Swimsuit, bra cups: Step 9.

Notes of Special Interest

All zippers sold today fall into three basic categories. They are either Invisible Zippers, Conventional Zippers, or Special Purpose Zippers.

Of the three, the **Invisible Zipper** is the newest and the most different closure development to come upon the home sewing scene. It is also becoming a very popular fastener because, once applied, the Invisible Zipper is absolutely inconspicuous. The zipper opening looks and acts just like a seam. The only telltale sign is the tiny pull tab at the top.

Conventional Zippers are those familiar fasteners you've been using for quite some time. If you want the look of a Lapped or Centered Zipper Application by hand or machine, this is the zipper to use. It is suitable for all types of fabrics and for all garment areas.

Special Purpose Zippers are those zippers which have been designed with a very specific function in mind. Their use is usually limited to a particular garment area. Included in this group are Separating Zippers and Trouser Zippers.

Within these three categories are a wide assortment of zippers that can be used in any number of ways. However, one fundamental fact remains: all are made with either nylon coils or metal teeth.

Nylon Zippers are:

Highly heat resistant to 450°F. This is comparable to a high

197

cotton setting on most irons. When using a linen temperature setting, we suggest placing a press cloth over the zipper for added protection.

Light, flexible, and strong because the coils are securely woven or stitched onto the zipper tape. Separation of coils from tape is not possible.

Washable and dry cleanable.

Compatible to most fabrics because the tape shrinkage is comparable to the majority of fabrics available.

Self-healing—When fabric or threads catch in coils they can be released. Bend zipper in half, pinch fold tightly, twist to open, then zip down and zip up.

Easy running due to a specially engineered slider.

Permanently dyed tapes and coils to assure color consistency.

Metal Zippers are:

Flexible and strong—Nylon zippers are preferred by most women, but for those home sewers who want metal zippers, they too, are available in Conventional and Invisible types. In addition, Separating Zippers are made in both light and heavy weights so you can select just the right zipper for your garment.

ZIPPER SELECTION AND YOU

Once you have decided what type of zipper and application is best for your garment, there is still one further consideration — your figure. If your pattern recommends a 22 inch zipper, but you are short, consider using a shorter length for a better proportion and comfort. On the otherhand, a taller girl may need the longer zipper for convenience when dressing or undressing.

Width of hips and derriére should also influence zipper selection especially for pants and skirts. Think about the room you will need to get in and out of the garment before purchasing your zipper.

Also, consider the design of the garment. For example, a skirt and jacket combination may lose some of its appeal if the zipper in the skirt shows below the jacket hem. Why not use two shorter zippers applied in two seams or an *Invisible Zipper* which would be completely inconspicuous?

Courtesy of Talon Educational Service

CHARTING YOUR ZIPPER COURSE

STYLE	LENGTHS	TYPE	USES	SUITABLE FABRICS	APPLI-CATION	SPECIAL NOTES
Invisible	7", 9", 12", 14", 16", 18", 20", 22".	Zephyr, Metal	All garments any location	All fabrics except very high or looped pile	Invisible seamlike-closure	Machine stitched only. Use Invisible Zipper Foot.
Skirt or Neckline	7", 9"	Zephyr, Metal	Skirts, pants	All fabrics	Lapped, Centered, Decorative, Exposed	Machine or hand stitched
Dress or Neckline	12", 14"	Zephyr, Metal	Dress underarm	All fabrics		
Neckline	4*, 5*, 6",10*, 16", 18", 20", 22", 24", 30*, 36*	Zephyr, Metal	Sleeves, children's wear, dresses, sportswear	All fabrics		
Separating Lightweight	10", 12", 14", 16", 18", 20", 22"	Metal	Sweaters, jackets	All fabrics	Lapped, Centered, Decorative, Exposed	Zipper opens at bottom end.
Separating Heavyweight	14", 16", 18", 20", 22", 24"	Metal	Jackets, coats, capes	All fabrics		
Trouser	11"	Metal	Jeans, pants, shorts	All fabrics	Fly type	Can be cut to fit shorter length zipper placket.
Big-Zip Neckline	5", 18", 20", 22"	Metal	Sportswear	All fabrics	Exposed	Ring pull tab.

*Not available in metal

Courtesy of Talon Educational Service

199

Before Application

Q. When should I apply the zipper?

A. In most instances you will find it easier to apply the zipper before other seams are joined. You will be working with flat, smaller pieces of fabric instead of an entire garment.

Q. What zipper application is best for my garment?

A. Weight of fabric, garment design, and convenience determine which of the following three basic zipper applications is most practical.

1. Invisible Application

□ Completely invisible from the right side except for the tiny pull tab

□ Ideal for front applications or those special garments where seeing the zipper would detract from the design

□ Suitable for all fabrics except those with a very high pile or looped surface

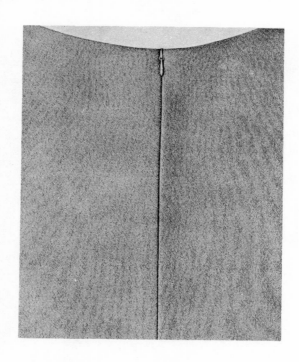

2. Lapped Application

□ Ideal for light to medium-weight fabrics

□ Completely conceals zipper at back or side openings
□ Results in reduced gapping at waistline

3. Centered Application
□ Ideal for heavy or pile fabrics—reduces bulk in zipper area
□ Symmetrical appearance best suited for center back or front openings
□ Suggested for design features such as slashed openings, wrist openings, and pleats

Q. When is a Hand Application used?

A. Hand finishing a zipper application gives a custom touch to your garment. This couturier look is preferred by many, regardless of type of fabric used. Both Lapped and Centered Applications can be sewn by hand.

A number of fabrics lend themselves to a hand finished zipper in order to be more flexible and less conspicuous than can be accomplished by machine stitching. For example:

□ Napped and Pile Fabrics such as velvet, velveteen, fur fabric, and wool

□ Knit Fabrics that are very loosely knitted such as a hand knit

□ Hard Surface and Sheer Fabrics such as taffeta, lace, crepe, organdy, organza, and chiffon

Q. Can I use a Neckline Zipper for an application that is closed at both top and bottom?

A. Yes. However, it is suggested that the tape ends be sewn together above the slider first. When doing final stitching of Lapped or Centered Application, continue stitching across the top of the zipper opening as you did across the bottom.

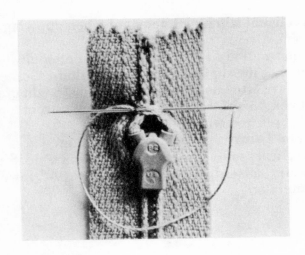

Q. How is a Separating Zipper applied?

A. Centered or Lapped Application methods are used to apply Separating Zippers. Appropriate facing techniques are given in the pattern instructions.

Q. What do I do if seam allowances are too narrow?

A. For a good application, a minimum of ⅝ inch seam allowance is needed. Narrow seam allowances should be widened with matching *Seam Binding*.

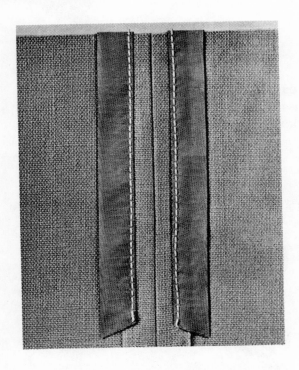

Q. Is directional stitching important when applying a Conventional Zipper?

A. Our instructions show stitching directionally on Lapped Applications but not on Centered Applications. Centered Applications are more often used in seams cut on straight grain such as the center back; therefore, stitching the zipper from top to bottom can be accomplished without stretching.

Q. How can I turn a corner while stitching?

A. Pivoting will assure perfect corners every time. Simply leave needle in fabric, raise zipper foot, pivot fabric 90°, lower foot, and continue stitching.

Q. How can I stitch straight past the slider?

A. When sewing past the slider, position the pull tab upward and tilt slider on its side.

Q. When should an underlay be used?

A. To protect delicate skin or undergarments, place a piece of grosgrain ribbon behind the zipper. (This is a particularly good idea for the metal zippers.) Cut ribbon 1" longer than opening. Finish one end and place it at top of zipper. Stitch one side of ribbon edge to left seam allowance and tack the lower end of the ribbon to the seam allowances. Place a small snap at free upper corner.

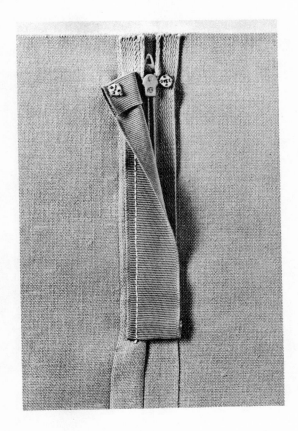

Q. What are the important zipper pressing techniques?

A. □ Always close zipper before pressing or ironing.

□ Before applying zipper, press out any fold marks.

□ Use a tailor's ham when pressing a zipper applied in a curved seam. This will preserve the shape of the garment.

□ Use a press cloth over zipper area when pressing on the right side to prevent shine and imprint of the zipper teeth.

Q. Is staystitching necessary at zipper openings?

A. Staystitching is not necessary on the straight grain unless your fabric is very stretchy or loosely woven. For control, stay-stitch curved or bias zipper openings with a line of regular machine stitches just inside the seamline in the seam allowance.

Q. Is pinning or basting really necessary?
A. Type of fabric used or inexperience of the sewer may indicate a need for pinning or basting.
Q. What is Zipper Adhesive and how can it help me?
A. It is a quick and easy aid to position zippers for application. The double-sided adhesive strip eliminates the need for pinning or basting. It is extremely helpful when matching plaids and stripes. In addition, it greatly reduces the puckering of fabric that may occur because it stabilizes the zipper tape to the fabric.

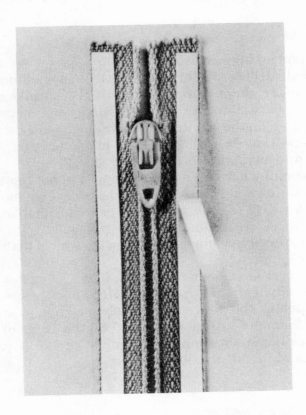

Q. How can I reduce bulk at cross seams?
A. Press the seam allowances according to the pattern instruction. Then clip the seam allowances to the stitching line ¾" from either side of the opening. Press open and trim to ⅛," as shown. Insert zipper and hand tack seam allowances.

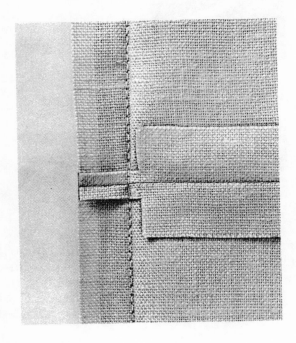

Q. Is preshrinking necessary?

A. A small degree of shrinkage has been included in most zippers to make them compatible with the shrinkage of most fabrics sold today. However, we would suggest preshrinking your zipper if you are in the habit or preshrinking your fabric or if you intend to sew a fabric with shrinkage of 1% or less.

Q. How do I preshrink a zipper?

A. Preshrink by immersing closed zipper in hot tap water for a few minutes. Roll zipper in a towel to absorb excess moisture and allow it to air dry. Lightly press zipper before application. For maximum shrinkage, repeat process.

Q. Will a special machine attachment give me a better application?

A. Zipper feet have been designed to give an easier and more professional application. For an *Invisible Zipper*, a special foot is required, such as the New Invisible Zipper Foot. A special feature, the "Diamond" head protrusion at the front of the foot, assures a perfect application every time. The foot is suitable for both nylon and metal Invisible Zippers.

For all other zippers use an adjustable zipper foot. It permits stitching on either side of the zipper. It should be adjusted so that no part of the foot rides on the zipper coil and that the needle is centered exactly in notch of foot.

Q. How is zipper length measured?
A. With zipper closed, zipper length is measured from the top of the slider down to the bottom stop.

During Application

Q. Are there any secrets to stitching straight when applying a Conventional Zipper?
A. Yes. A sewing guideline is woven into the zipper tape to aid in straight stitching. Follow it when stitching on the wrong side, or baste along it as a guide to follow when stitching on the right side. It also assures adequate space between the stitching line and zipper coil or teeth for easy movement of the slider.

Courtesy of Talon Educational Service

Just as there's a way to use thread while hand sewing, the same applies to machine stitching.

Are you ready to sew?

Check your machine to see that:

□ Threading is correct.

□ Bobbin loading is even.

□ Take-up lever is at the highest point to avoid jamming.

□ Both thread ends are pulled toward the back of the presser foot.

□ Pressure and tension are loosened slightly for synthetic threads.

Then, before stitching:

□ Lower the needle into the fabric.

□ Lower the presser foot.

□ Begin stitching and try to maintain an even pace, even if a slow one. Uneven spurts of speed will result in uneven stitching.

Is the stitch quality satisfactory?

If the stitches are skipped:

□ Needle type is not related to fabric, e.g., Ballpoint or Yellow Band needle for knits.

□ Needle groove is clogged with residue from fabric finishes or lint from fabric.

□ Needle is incorrectly inserted.

□ Needle is bent.

□ Needle and thread sizes are not related.

If fabric around stitching is puckered:

□ The needle tension is too tight.

□ Both needle and bobbin tension are too tight for fabric type.

□ The needle is too heavy for the fabric.

□ The stitch size is too large for the fabric.

If stitching is loose:

□ Thread tension is too slack. Adjust tensions, using test for a balanced stitch.

If your stitching looks unbalanced:
- Stitch a seam on the bias grain through two layers of fabric.
- Pull layers from both ends of stitching until a thread breaks.
- If top thread breaks, loosen tension dial; if bottom thread breaks, tighten dial.
- Do not adjust the bobbin tension until you have exhausted all other methods of obtaining a perfect stitch.

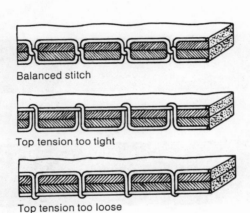

Balanced stitch

Top tension too tight

Top tension too loose

If the thread breaks check for these features on your machine:
- Bent or blunt needle.
- Needle incorrectly inserted.
- Needle groove or eye having sharp edges.
- Needle groove clogged with deposits from fabric lint or fabric finishes.
- Size of needle and thread not related.
- Area under throat plate clogged with lint.
- Tension of needle or bobbin too tight.
- Incorrect threading.
- Throat plate hole or thread guide rough.
- Bobbin case inserted incorrectly.
- Bobbin unevenly wound or too full.

Courtesy of Talon Educational Service

Standard tapes and braids are available in packaged form. Most are utilitarian in use and classic in design. Decorative trims can be purchased by the yard.

Seam Binding (Woven Edge) is made of 100% rayon. It is ½ inch wide with two woven edges on the straight grain. Available in many colors, Seam Binding is used to finish hem and seam allowance edges, extend seam allowances, or act as a stay strip.

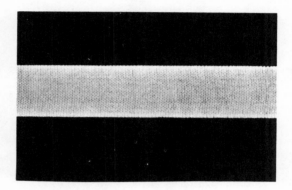

Lace Seam Binding is made of 100% nylon. It is ⅝ inch wide with one straight edge and one scalloped edge so that it will conform to any shape—straight or curved. It is a particularly elegant finish for hems, seams, facings, and lingerie. Its stretch quality makes it ideal for knit type fabrics.

Bias Seam Tape (Folded) is cut on the bias grain and is made of 100% nylon. It is ½ inch wide after the edges have been folded. It serves the same functions as woven edge *Seam Binding* and is particlarly suited to curved hems and edges.

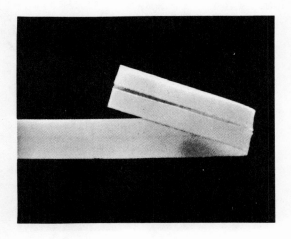

Bias Tape (Single Fold) is a versatile bias strip made of 100% cotton. It has two folded edges and is ½ inch wide after folding. It is used to bind straight or curved edges both functionally and decoratively.

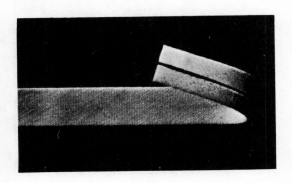

Bias Tape (Double Fold) is also made of 100% cotton. It is ¼ inch wide after folding. Double Fold Bias Tape is exactly like *Single Fold Bias Tape* in form and function except it is folded again to become half the width. For ease of application, the fold is made slightly off center so that one side is wider than the other. Note: The narrower half should always be on the top portion of the application so the bottom half will automatically be stitched during application.

Fold-over Braid is a prefolded braid for binding edges. One side of the braid is slightly narrower to facilitate application. Woven on the bias or knitted in cotton, polyester, or rayon, Fold-over Braid can be shaped to fit most curves.

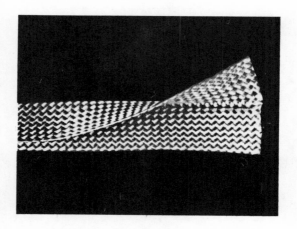

Loop Braid is a cotton braid that has one straight edge and one decorative edge and comes in one width, ½ inch. It can be used in straight and curved applications as an edging or a banding.

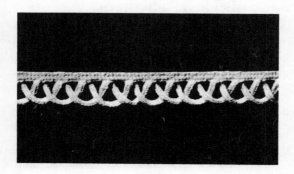

Middy Braid is braid that can be used singly or in multiples for outlining monograms and designs of a straight-line nature, and as a drawstring. Middy Braid is available 3/16 inch wide, and is made of rayon-covered cotton.

Piping is a cotton trim that can be used for a fine decorative seam accent. Piping is ⅜ inch wide and is made in several fashion colors. It can be used as an edging or inserted into any major structural seam that needs highlighting.

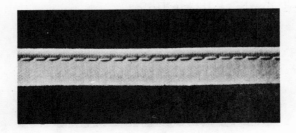

Rickrack can be used as an edging or a banding on many types of apparel and home decorating projects. Rickrack is made of no-iron mercerized cotton and is sold in ⅛ inch (Baby), ½ inch (Regular), and ¾ inch (Jumbo) widths. Regular Rickrack is also made of non-tarnishable metallic yarn.

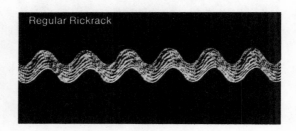

Shell Braid is made of no-iron mercerized cotton covered by non-tarnishable metallic yarn. Shell Braid is available in ½ inch widths for use as an edging or banding in single or multiple treatments.

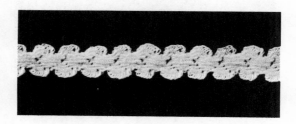

Soutache Braid is a braid with an indentation in the center that can be used as a convenient location for stitching the braid in place. Being very narrow, ⅛ inch, Soutache Braid is suitable for intricate curvilinear patterns. Made of rayon-covered cotton, it can be used singly or in multiples.

Bias Tape (Wide) is made of 100% cotton and is ⅞ inch wide after folding. It can be used to bind or trim the edges of heavier fabrics as well as serve as a facing substitute or casing fabric.

Hem Facing is cut on the bias grain and is available in both 100% cotton and 100% acetate taffeta. It is 2 inches wide after folding. Use it as a hem facing or as a facing substitute.

Wide lace is made from 100% nylon. It is a stretchable decorative edge lace 1¾ inches wide. Its feminine pattern matches the motif of narrow stretch *Lace Seam Binding*. It is designed for use as a hem facing, as a hem finish on lingerie, or as a decorative trim.

Twill Tape is made from 100% cotton, in black and white only. It is available in ¼ inch, ½ inch, ¾ inch, and 1 inch widths for use as drawstrings, stay strips, or button reinforcements.

Blanket Binding is woven from 100% acetate satin. It is made on the straight grain and available in both 2 inch and 2⅞ inch folded widths.

Courtesy of Talon Educational Service

Index